T0308918

ON THE PORCH

BRAD AND MICHELE MOORE ROOTS MUSIC SERIES

ON THE PORCH

Life and Music in Terlingua, Texas

W. CHASE PEELER

UNIVERSITY OF TEXAS PRESS Austin

Requests for permission to reproduce material from this work should
be sent to:
Permissions
University of Texas Press
P.O. Box 7819
Austin, TX 78713-7819
utpress.utexas.edu/rp-form

All song lyrics quoted in the text are attributed to their artists
(when known) in the endnotes.

All photographs appearing in the text are by the author.

♾ The paper used in this book meets the minimum requirements of
ANSI/NISO Z39.48-1992 (R1997) (Permanence of Paper).

Library of Congress Cataloging Data

Names: Peeler, W. Chase, author.
Title: On the Porch : life and music in Terlingua, Texas / W. Chase
    Peeler.
Description: First edition. | Austin : University of Texas Press, 2021. |
    Includes bibliographical references and index.
Identifiers: LCCN 2021000645 (print) | LCCN 2021000646 (ebook)
ISBN 978-1-4773-2364-9 (hardcover)
ISBN 978-1-4773-2365-6 (library ebook)
ISBN 978-1-4773-2366-3 (non-library ebook)
Subjects: LCSH: Music—Texas—Terlingua. | Gentrification—
    Texas—Terlingua. | Terlingua (Tex.) | Terlingua (Tex.)—Social
    life and customs. | Mexican-American Border Region—Political
    aspects.
Classification: LCC F394.T285 P44 2021 (print) | LCC F394.T285
    (ebook) | DDC 976.4/932—dc23
LC record available at https://lccn.loc.gov/2021000645
LC ebook record available at https://lccn.loc.gov/2021000646

doi:10.7560/323649

FOR TERLINGUA,
WITH AFFECTION

CONTENTS

ON THE PORCH

ON THE PORCH

IT'S AROUND THREE O'CLOCK in the afternoon when I decide to make my way up to the Porch. Into the back of the car I throw my guitar and a pair of saxophones. I don't expect to play the latter, but I put them in anyway because I remember some advice Moses gave me during my first week in town.

"One thing you need to learn about Terlingua," he told me, "when you come to the Porch, bring every instrument you own." He may have been exaggerating, but he does have a point. The Porch is the social and musical center of town, the place where local musicians go to sing and play almost every day of the week. You can never be sure what's going to happen until you get there: you might be one of a dozen musicians or you might be alone; you might hear old-time fiddle music or western swing, country, folk, or rock 'n' roll; you might find yourself in the middle of a circle of song-writers performing in turns or a blues jam where everyone jumps in all at once. The music can be a struggle one day and transcendent the next. A wise musician comes prepared for any possibility.

I turn out of BJ's RV Park and begin heading west on Highway 170, the famous "River Road" that follows the Rio Grande as it traverses the canyon country of the Big Bend through far West Texas. A mile's drive brings me to the main

Ghost Town turnoff where a cluster of signs announces food and lodging to passersby. An iron marker placed by the State Historical Survey Committee informs readers that the Terlingua Ghost Town was once home to the Chisos Mining Company, a mercury mining operation that started in the late 1890s but went bust shortly after World War II. Farther up the road, a wooden sign with peeling paint informs visitors that the Ghost Town is listed in the National Register of Historic Places. The designation is certainly deserved as most of the ruins and other artifacts from the original settlement are still here. Still, referring to this place as a "ghost town" feels like a bit of a misnomer these days considering that at least a hundred people now call it home.

Driving into the Ghost Town can be a sensory overload for first-time visitors, as it looks like a weird mishmash of historical site, shantytown, wildlife area, trailer park, primitive campground, art installation, tourist trap, and junkyard. Travelers are greeted at the entrance by a life-size replica of a pirate ship and another of a submarine, both built to look like they have been partially submerged underground. Up the road on the right is a pickup-sized piece of artwork resembling a giant mosquito or some other winged creature, fashioned out of old car parts and bits of metal and swiveling high on a pole. Farther out, a white cabin boat, perhaps twenty-five feet long, rests on its hull among the cacti with no evidence to suggest how or why it arrived in the desert. On the left, a picturesque cemetery perched on the edge of a deep ravine contains crumbling gravestones and wooden crosses, many of them unmarked, from the past 120 years or so. Clustered in the northeast corner, a handful of newer headstones show that the site is still in use. In a small community garden adjacent to the cemetery, rows of vegetables break up the monotony of the desert flora.

As I proceed across the undulating terrain, remnants of buildings made of stones and adobe bricks the same color as the earth appear and disappear among the creosote bushes.

Some have been reduced to disintegrated outlines by vandalism or by their constant exposure to the harsh desert sun and wind. Others are better preserved, and these have been refurbished and reoccupied by a new wave of residents who began repopulating the Ghost Town in the late 1970s. Many of the more recent arrivals have chosen to bring their homes with them—an old school bus, perhaps, or a prefabricated metal structure. Here and there my eye catches the faded glint of an old Airstream trailer interspersed among the earthen dwellings, their neglected silver exteriors looking more like old coins than mirrors. Newer buildings dot the landscape as well, some made with conventional materials and others from adobe, old tires, beer cans and plaster, or whatever else happened to be both inexpensive and readily available. A few of the newest houses have yet to shed their protective Tyvek cocoons. These days there is always someone building.

The main road used to be dirt, but it was paved about a decade before I arrived in town. Many locals look at such signs of "progress" and shake their heads. On a few occasions, I have heard someone proclaim, "I was here before the road was paved," which sounds like something not worth boasting about, but being able to say so puts a person in more select company than you might think. Even fewer people can say they were here back in the 1970s and 80s, when the Starlight Theatre was still a roofless ruin that served as an after-work hangout for a handful of river guides. It's a familiar refrain, one that can be heard throughout small-town America: *Times are changing. Gone are the good ol' days.* It sounds like a cliché until you've lived it yourself. Many Terlingua residents have already said those words about other places—that's one reason why they moved to a "ghost town" in the middle of the desert.

The road ends at a complex of ruins in the center of the Ghost Town that have been remodeled and turned into businesses: on the right, the Starlight Theatre (a restaurant and bar); on the left, the Terlingua Trading Company (a souvenir shop); and in between, a long, covered area connecting the two, known locally as "the Porch." The pavement erodes into dirt once the road reaches the parking lot, and I have to steer my way through a handful of cars that are parked willy-nilly. (There are no lines painted in the lot and tourists are not always adept at parking in orderly rows.) Fortunately, it's still early in the afternoon and the rush hasn't hit yet, so I have my choice of several spots right in front of the Porch. I can already see most of the regulars: Judy, Ed, Clem, Mike, Big Hat Dave, Ralph, Catfish, and Shawn are all here, as well as a handful of people I don't recognize, though no one is playing music yet. I get out of the car, leaving the doors unlocked with the keys in the ignition and my instruments in the backseat, and walk down the Porch saying hello to everyone. I pass the stand where the Porch guitar sits, swing open the big wooden door to the Trading Company, and head to the back room where I grab two Lone Star longnecks out of the refrigerator. No one is at the register but the beer list is on the counter, so I scroll down the column of names scribbled on the large yellow notepad until I find my own and see that I still have four beers left from the last time I bought a six-pack. I cross off numbers 4 and 3 next to my name and walk back outside.

I take a seat next to Clem on one of the long wooden benches that stretch the length of the Porch and hand him one of the beers. It is warmer than usual for March, and the bench and the plastered adobe wall at my back feel cool in the dry heat of the afternoon. During the summer months, when the temperature regularly exceeds 110 degrees Fahrenheit, these benches provide a shady refuge for the people who live here without air conditioning, which is most of the population. As I take a swig and set the bottle on the bench beside me, I look down and notice that the edge of the bench closest to the wall is more rounded than the outside edge, worn smooth from repeated contact with the legs of decades of Porch sitters.[1] Someone must have thought

The Terlingua Porch, with the Starlight Theatre on the right, 2016.

to rotate the benches at intervals so they would wear more evenly, not unlike the way you're supposed to rotate the tires on a car. It's a good idea—they look like they've been here a long time, as do the walls with their peeling paint and eroding plaster, the smooth-worn brick and stone tile under- foot, the patchwork metal roof that leaks when it rains, and the slowly disintegrating wooden beams that hold the roof in place. I have seen a handful of photographs of the Porch from the 1960s and 70s and it doesn't appear that much has changed in the intervening decades. That's part of the appeal.

As the minutes pass, a steady trickle of cars begins filling the parking lot, and before long I spot Mark Lewis's white two-door pickup creeping up the road from the highway. He pulls up in front of the Porch and gets out, grabbing his fiddle and mandolin cases from the back seat. I get up to fetch my guitar, and by the time I return, Mark is already seated on the bench tuning his fiddle. He is dressed in his standard at- tire: a plain white t-shirt, sleeves cut off at the shoulders to reveal muscular arms sculpted by years of rowing a raft; shirt tucked into dark denim shorts, cut long but rolled up over the knees; Chaco sandals, sunglasses, and a black skull cap with white skull-and-crossbones pattern, tied in the back with tag ends flowing over a short ponytail of graying hair. Like many longtime locals, Mark has the sunbaked look of a desert dweller that sets him immediately apart from the more casual visitors to the Big Bend. He hands me a fresh Lone Star as I grab a folding chair and sit down to face him.

"Are you telling me you haven't been playing yet?" he asks, looking at the closed guitar case in my hand.

"Not yet," I answer. "I was waiting for someone else to show up."

"Well, dammit, someone's got to get it started!" Mark smiles. "How about the 'Boatman's Song'?" It's one he learned recently so he has been calling it often for practice. I finish tuning my guitar and wait for him to play "potatoes," a distinct four-beat rhythm used in old-time fiddle music to signal that the tune is starting, and together we launch in, Mark playing the melody and me providing the rhythmic *boom-chuck* guitar accompaniment typical for this style. The accompaniment is relatively straightforward, with chords coming in predictable succession, so occasionally I spice things up, only half intentionally, by throwing in little rhythmic hiccups of syncopation here and there. When I do this, Mark immediately glances up from his fiddle, and in my mind I hear him reminding me: *The guitar is the foundation, it carries the tunes. . . . Don't play any of that syncopation that singer-songwriters play. . . . You are the drummer in this music, it has to be steady.* I rein it in and focus on locking into the rhythm.

We play another fiddle tune and another. When I botch the chords, Mark helps me get back on track by calling them aloud while he plays, sometimes using numbers ("one . . . four . . . one . . . five . . .") and other times using letters ("G . . . F . . . C . . . G . . ."). He ends each tune by lifting his foot to signal the last time through the form. When we finish a tune that was really clicking, he smiles and says, "Thank you, that was a good ride." Mark always thanks me when we play together. He doesn't get many opportunities to play these tunes with an accompanist, despite the fact that "there's a guitarist under every rock in this town," as one resident informed me when I moved here. Terlingua is brimming with singer-songwriters, but only a handful of local musicians have shown any interest in learning old-time fiddle music, and this has frustrated Mark at times. When I accepted his offer to teach me the style—a tradition I had long wanted to learn—it led to a quick friendship.

After four or five tunes, Mark sets his fiddle down and begins rolling a cigarette with practiced motions, looking more at the horizon than at his hands.

"Man, what a gorgeous day," he says as he leans back against the wall. "There wasn't a breath of wind on the river today, made for *real* easy paddling. Yeah, it was awesome." I get up from the folding chair and take a seat next to him so I can see the desert panorama, and for a while the two of us sit in silence as we admire the view. The landscape here possesses such immediacy that it often feels like a participant in the conversation. This is especially true on the Porch: it is one of the best places in Terlingua—indeed, one of the best places in the entire Big Bend—from which to view the Chisos Mountains to the east. Even though we're only eight miles from the boundary of Big Bend National Park, it's an additional twenty or so miles to the Chisos massif, and from this vantage point you can see the entire range from end to end. The scene reminds me of the view from the back of a concert hall: how all the rows slope gradually down as they progress forward so that every seat is visible, until suddenly, at the lowest point of the room, the stage juts abruptly upward into a place of prominence so that it becomes the focal point for the entire hall. Sitting on the Porch benches, the Chisos appear as the orchestra, and the entire desert foreground slopes downward toward their base so that every butte and arroyo between the Porch and the mountains seem to be laid clearly in view. I can't help but wonder if the original architects had this scenery in mind, or if the building's orientation was intended for some more utilitarian purpose: to catch the warmth of the winter sunrise in the southeast, perhaps, or to provide a view overlooking activities in the town below. At any rate, these days the Porch is famous for its view, and its notoriety is well deserved.

Today is a clear spring day and visibility is good, which is typical for this part of the country, and all the park landmarks are within view: Emory Peak, Casa Grande, the Window, Mule Ears, Elephant Tusk. Off to the right and just out of sight behind Reed Plateau, a great V marks where the Rio Grande cuts through Santa Elena Canyon in the Mesa de Anguila. Even the Pinos Mountains are clearly visible where they stand in isolation a hundred miles south of the river into Mexico. The Chisos are a washed-out ruddy brown this time of day, but their shadows have already started to elongate, making their wrinkly texture more plainly visible. In a few hours, the setting sun at our backs will cast its changing light on the desert canvas before us, painting it in gradually deepening shades of pink, orange, red, purple, and blue.

"Looks like it's gonna be a good one today," I remark. A response comes from someone to my right.

"Only place I know where people watch the sun set in the east." I smile and take another swig of beer. I remember hearing someone else say this when I first arrived in town, but at the time I didn't appreciate the deeper significance of what sounds like a straightforward statement. After all, if it weren't for the national park and the tourism it brings, Terlingua probably would have remained uninhabited once its mining heyday ended. A comment that points to the relationship between Terlingua and the Chisos Mountains— the crown jewel of the national park—would thus seem to warrant no further explanation. But the more time I spend

The Chisos Mountains as seen from the Terlingua Porch, 2013.

in Terlingua, the more I come to realize that these eastern
sunsets hold symbolic meaning for many who live here.

In the years since its rebirth, the Terlingua Ghost Town
has developed a reputation as a haven for people who drift
at the margins of mainstream American society—a reputation that seems fitting for a town that is also geographically
situated at one of the remotest margins of the contiguous
United States. Terlingua is a town that is self-consciously
other, a place where weirdness is cultivated and celebrated.
Locals will tell you that it takes a special kind of person to
live here. Most residents live partially or entirely off-grid, re-
lying on solar power and rainwater collection to satisfy their
needs. Some people forego electricity and running water entirely. One Ghost Town resident lives in a cave and has done
so comfortably for more than twenty-five years. The nearest
airport with any kind of commercial service is 238 miles
away. The nearest stoplight is 65 miles away in Mexico or
150 miles away in Texas. Making a life in Terlingua, because

of its isolation, has always taken a commitment to simple living and a willingness to forego many of the conveniences and amenities that characterize life in a developed nation. Not surprisingly, such relative hardships have long ensured that the population in Terlingua remains small and extremely close-knit. Terlinguans speak with reverence about their spirit of community, a bond that is cultivated through the shared experience of remote living in a harsh and unforgiving environment. It is a feeling that most locals say they were only able to discover once they dropped out of the rat race that is urban life and moved to the desert.

All this is to say that when Terlinguans gaze out at the Chisos Mountains and proclaim, "Out here, we watch the sun set in the east," they are talking about more than geography. The eastern sunset is a symbolic and celebratory affirmation of Terlingua as an alternative social and cultural space. *In Terlingua, we do things a little differently.*

"WHY DON'T YOU SING ONE?" Mark says to me after we've been sitting for a while. I think about it for a moment.

"How about a Townes song?" I ask. "Let's do 'Don't You Take It Too Bad.' I do it in E-flat, starts on the five." He picks up his mandolin and I launch into a short melodic introduction before beginning the first verse of the song. Mark finds his way along the neck of the instrument and through the patterns in the new key, an uncommon one for string players, but once he gets his fingers going he begins inserting snippets of melody into the breaks in my singing.

Partway through the second verse, I hear someone whistle to my right and look up to see Jeffro and Sha (pronounced "Shaye") approaching from the direction of the Starlight Theatre. Sha radiates enthusiasm, from her sprightly pigtails to her colorful sundress and cowboy boots to the way she waves at us with both hands. Jeffro, ever calm and casual, smiles a subtler greeting, his guitar in one hand and his cane in the other. I pause the song by vamping on the one chord while we all exchange a few punctuated hellos. Sha bends down as she passes to hug me around the neck from behind, being careful not to hit the guitar as I keep time, before taking a seat next to Catfish a few feet away. Jeffro lowers himself into the folding chair next to me, and as I resume singing, he takes out his guitar and begins tuning up.

"Take it, Mark!" I call after the third verse. Mark crescendos so that his mandolin is now the most prominent voice, and he takes over the main melody, embellishing it here and there as he goes. As he nears the end of the form, I lean over to get Jeffro's attention. "You want one?" Jeffro nods and takes the lead as Mark wraps up his solo and reverts to a quieter strumming pattern. We take it once more through the form before I repeat the first verse and gesture with my foot to conclude the song. Sha and several others clap, and Judy yells "Ayeeeeeeeee!" as we wrap up the song and reach for our beers.

"Batter up, Jeffro," Mark says. Jeffro strums a few chords to make sure he's in tune before launching into "Northeast Texas Women" by Willis Alan Ramsey. I grab the capo off my guitar and use it to play a backbeat rhythm on the neck of my beer bottle. Clem, who up until this point has been listening in silence, gets up from his seat and returns with the washboard that he leaves just inside the entrance to the Trading Company, and he too begins to play rhythm. As the song picks up momentum, a handful of tourists walking down the Porch begin slowing down to watch us as they pass. A few reach for their cameras and begin taking photographs, and Sha stands up from the bench to take some pictures with her smartphone. When Jeffro gets to the line, "Kisses that are sweeter than cactus," he instead sings, "Kisses that are sweeter than Catfish." Sha has anticipated this alteration and sings it along with Jeffro. As she does, she motions to Catfish who is still sitting a few feet away with a contented look on his face, skinny legs crossed at the knees and foot tapping where it is suspended in the air.

"*Nothing* is sweeter than Catfish!" Sha says as she reclaims her seat beside him. Catfish remains silent, but his eyes sparkle as he smiles through his beard. Like most Porch sitters, he alternates between listening to the music and conversing with friends. The atmosphere on the Porch is informal—this is not a "concert" in the traditional sense of the word—so there is no expected code of conduct for the audience. Here, talking is allowed, and cell phones need not be silenced. This informality extends to the musicians as well, as they too drift in and out of conversation while the music is being played. Musicians come and go, playing a little or a lot, moving seamlessly from performer to audience member and back to performer until the line between "performer" and "audience" becomes blurred and the terms no longer seem appropriate.

Jeffro leans back in his chair and holds up his leg to end the song. Some applause and hollering, a bit more enthusiastic this time, emanates from the Porch. A tourist wearing a bright blue polo shirt tucked into ironed khaki shorts reaches down and throws a ten-dollar bill into Jeffro's guitar case, which is sitting open in the middle of the circle of musicians.

"Y'all are great," he says to the group. "Y'all could be playing on 5th Street in Austin."

"Well, most of us *escaped* from Austin," Clem says. "Too many fuckin' monkeys and they're all in a hurry." He cracks his knuckles and replaces the empty can in his koozie with a full one. The man in the polo shirt laughs awkwardly.

"Well, anyway, y'all sound great. Do any of you ever play in the Starlight?"

"I'm playing there tonight," says Clem.

"But you know," Mark interjects, "you don't need a stage or an audience to play music. That's not why we play. Music shouldn't be about *me me me me me*. It should be about *WE*." He gestures to signify the group.

The man smiles politely. "Well, thank you for the music. We enjoyed listening to y'all." Jeffro thanks him as he walks away, and Mark picks up the ten dollars and takes it inside to buy a six-pack to share among the musicians. Jeffro leans forward in his chair and holds the guitar at arm's length in Clem's direction. "Clem, you got one?"

Clem doesn't respond immediately. "Hmm. . . . No, I better not," he finally answers. "I still gotta play inside later." He looks at me and a grin stretches across his whiskered face. "It's like, 'These old hands can't handle as much playin' as they used to,' right?" He laughs and holds up his hands in front of his chest, opening and closing them to demonstrate their decreased mobility. A three-hour show is a lot for him these days, but he still plays the Starlight every Tuesday night, as he has for years. Clem wired the place for electricity back when it first opened for business in 1991, so today he enjoys an unwritten contract for a weekly performance.

Clem eventually goes inside to start his gig, but other musicians soon arrive to take his place on the benches. We follow a loose rotation, taking turns leading songs and playing solos. The membership of the group changes constantly as musicians enter and exit, sometimes to grab another round of beers, sometimes to go into the Starlight for food, sometimes to talk to someone elsewhere on the Porch, and sometimes simply to listen. Nearby, Pat O'Bryan spends most of the afternoon chewing on a cigar while taking photographs of the musicians for his website chronicling the Terlingua music scene, but after some prodding, he eventually sits down to play some bluesy lead guitar behind the singers. Sometimes the tourists will bring their guitars and ask to sit in, but on most days the participants are locals who join without being prompted. The style of music fluctuates depending on who is leading at any given moment:

Webster plays a country song in the classic style of Hank Williams Sr.; Jeffro plays a soft and introspective original; I play a rowdy outlaw country song by Gary P. Nunn; Carol sings a slow and melancholy folk song about Terlingua's mining days; Mark plays a fiddle tune and then leads the group in a Grateful Dead classic; Chris delivers an emotional folk song in her haunting and unforgettable alto. Eventually, Charlotte shows up and takes the whole thing up a notch by backing up the singers on her viola and cello.

Alex and Marti Whitmore arrive for dinner as the sun nears the horizon, but they sit down to sing a few songs before they enter the Starlight. The Whitmores have an unmistakable sound when they perform as a duo: Alex plays precise finger-style guitar and sings in a clear, folky tenor, while Marti is a classically trained operatic soprano who accompanies her husband by drumming with brushes on an old threadbare suitcase. The first song they sing, an original titled "79852" after Terlingua's zip code, has become something of a local anthem. Cheers erupt immediately upon the first few chords, and when Alex and Marti arrive at the chorus, a handful of voices join in from across the Porch to sing along with the refrain:

> I found myself in the middle of nowhere
> I found myself in the middle of nowhere
> I found myself in 7-9-8-5-2

As the afternoon progresses into evening, the light show on the Chisos intensifies and the Porch gradually fills with people until it becomes a bustling hive of activity. To my right, a throng of tourists with drinks in hand mill around and converse while waiting for tables to open in the Starlight, and every now and then the hostess comes outside and yells a name: *Robert, party of four!* The rest of the Porch is filled with people sitting and standing, drinking beer and

cocktails, talking, laughing, sometimes yelling, taking pho-
tos of the Chisos and each other, and otherwise enjoying the
evening atmosphere. A few couples dance a two-step when
we happen to play a country song at about the right tempo.
Out in the parking lot, some locals play Hacky Sack, laughing
and hollering and jumping and trying their best to keep the
small footbag airborne without spilling their beers. Nearby,
a few others are hula-hooping, alternately selecting from a
dozen different-sized hoops that Shawn made from plumbing pipe and electrical tape. In the middle of everything, a
pack of dogs chase each other up, down, and off the Porch,
deftly weaving slalom-like between pairs of legs. I watch as
they streak past two tourists who look at each other inquisi-
tively while pointing to a wooden sign hanging conspicuously
from the roof: *No Dogs on the Porch.* Occasionally, all this
activity gets drowned out by bikers announcing their com-
ings and goings with revving engines, presumably for their
own amusement but much to the annoyance of everyone
else.

Everything is happening at once, and the music continues. We get louder and louder, weaving our rhythms into
the rhythms around us until it all becomes a single strand.
Finally, after reaching a high point of activity around dusk,
the Porch gradually begins to quiet down as everyone waiting for tables makes it inside. One by one, the musicians
begin packing up their instruments and leaving for the night.
Eventually, Mark and I are the only two musicians remaining. Our instruments are already in their cases, and we sit
facing east as we finish what's left of our beers. The Trading
Company is all locked up for the night, and over by its entrance the Porch guitar rests idly on its stand. The colors on
the Chisos have faded to blackness, but before long a new
light show will begin as the stars come out one by one and
the Milky Way appears, its entire length clearly visible like
a streak of powdered sugar flung across the sky. To our left,

a handful of people are sitting on the patio in front of the Starlight. Soft light and the sounds of Clem's amplified guitar come bleeding out the front door into the night.

"You know," Mark says, "when I first came to Terlingua, there were hardly any lights between here and the Chisos. *Man*, it was dark." He gazes out in silence for a while, as if he is trying to resurrect the image in his head. I try to picture it, too. Another longtime local once told me that it was like being on a boat on the ocean at night. Then Mark looks over at me and smiles. "Good tunes today, man. Thank you. Yeah, it was a *good* day on the Porch. One of the best days of music I've seen here in a long time." He drains his bottle, grabs his instruments, and stands up to leave. "Yeah, this was *fuuun*. But it's sad, you know. People in this town just don't play on the Porch like they used to."

I sit alone for a while longer, reflecting on Mark's final words as the taillights of his pickup bump and snake their way down the dirt road to his house.

I know he was thinking about more than music.

HUNDRED MILES FROM NOWHERE

You go south from Fort Davis
Until you come to the place
Where rainbows wait for the rain,
And the big river is kept in a stone box,
And the water runs uphill,
And the mountains float in the air,
Except at night when they go away
To play with other mountains
—UNKNOWN

A LITTLE MORE THAN HALFWAY through its passage from
the San Juan Mountains of Colorado to the Gulf of Mexico,
the Rio Grande briefly interrupts its southeasterly bearing,
veering north for about 130 miles before turning back and re-
suming its passage to the Gulf. It is a distinctive feature, one
that is easily identifiable on any map of North America. The
parched, mountainous, sparsely inhabited swath of Chihuahuan Desert contained within this crook is known as the Big
Bend Country of Texas. Its boundaries are debatable—the
region is as much an idea as a concretely defined place—
but by just about anyone's measure the Big Bend is huge:
more than twenty-five thousand square miles by a typical
estimate, making it considerably larger than nine US states
and nearly as large as West Virginia. The Big Bend is also the

least inhabited region in Texas, with a total population approaching only twenty-four thousand. This makes the population density of the Big Bend a scant 0.9 people per square mile. (The state of Alaska, by comparison, checks in at 1.3.)

Tucked away in the southernmost reaches of this vast country, about ten miles as the crow flies from the Rio Grande and forty miles upstream from where the river begins its northward turn, sits the Terlingua Ghost Town. First established in the late 1890s as a mining camp, Terlingua grew to become one of the largest producers of mercury in the world, and at its peak during World War I, it was home to more than two thousand people. The town was abandoned when the market for mercury collapsed following World War II, and it remained almost entirely uninhabited for the next thirty years. In the late 1970s, Terlingua was reborn when a handful of river guides set up shop in the Ghost Town's crumbling ruins and began offering commercial rafting trips on the Rio Grande. Today the town economy is fueled largely by tourism, thanks in no small part to its strategic position between two of the largest tracts of public land in the state: Big Bend Ranch State Park to the west and Big Bend National Park to the east.

During the Big Bend's mining period, a handful of distinct villages dotted the Terlingua area, each centered around the claims of a different mining company. The past four decades of steady population growth have caused these re-inhabited areas to gradually grow together. The name "Terlingua," which once referred specifically to the Ghost Town, now refers broadly to a large swath of South Brewster County stretching roughly forty highway miles from end to end.[1] Most of South County's population is concentrated in and around a handful of loosely connected areas: the Terlingua Ghost Town, a census-designated place (CDP) with an official population of 58; Study Butte CDP (pronounced "Stoody Byoot"), population 233; and Lajitas and Terlingua Ranch, neither of which registers in a search of the US Census website. No one believes in the accuracy of these figures because obtaining a precise tally of the area population would be prohibitively difficult. In fact, the two officials responsible for conducting the 2010 census in South Brewster County revealed in personal conversation with me that they had to search the area for houses by plane and horseback. Besides, even if an accurate census were possible, it would not be truly representative because most Terlinguans do not live in the Big Bend year-round. Most estimates put the de facto population somewhere in the neighborhood of fifteen hundred people during the peak season—roughly October through the end of April—and perhaps four or five hundred during the hot summer months when most seasonal residents retreat to cooler climates.

When considering its diminutive population and its isolation from urban Texas—300 miles from El Paso, 500 from Austin, 600 from Dallas, 650 from Houston—Terlingua might seem like one of the least likely places in the country to find music. Despite appearances, however, Terlingua residents have developed a vibrant music culture befitting a town one hundred times its size. In Terlingua, informal music making occurs on a daily basis, often multiple times and in multiple locations per day. Dozens of resident musicians perform gigs in a half-dozen local music venues, and it is not uncommon to have live music occurring in four or five places simultaneously. Terlingua music is not limited to live performance; remarkably, the town has had a full-service recording studio for more than twenty-five years—longer than it has had a school, a well-stocked grocery store, or even a public water utility. Local songwriters are numerous and prolific; they have created a rich repertoire of songs describing life in Terlingua from the perspectives of residents, and they perform these songs with fellow musicians in unconventional, genre-bending combinations unlikely to occur

anywhere else. Some local musicians even manage to make
a living from their craft despite living hundreds or thousands
of miles from the capital cities of the commercial music
industry.

When compared with most musical environments in the
United States, Terlingua stands out for being particularly
good at nurturing less experienced musicians. The town
boasts a long list of residents and visitors who have enjoyed
formative musical experiences in Terlingua, whether learning to play an instrument, writing an original song, recording
an album, participating in a jam for the first time, or even
performing a first-ever paying gig. It is standard practice
elsewhere in the country to segregate musicians by ability
level, but in Terlingua, beginners and advanced musicians
regularly perform alongside one another, both in jams and
onstage. Indeed, the opportunities and encouragement af-
forded to less experienced players are so great that many
people credit the unique musical climate of Terlingua for
driving their musical development.

In the United States, where public music making is often
considered the exclusive domain of the singularly "gifted" or
skilled, Terlingua stands out for the sheer number of people
of all ability levels who perform on a regular basis. For many
Terlinguans, music is a way of life: it is created for work and
for entertainment, in times of joy and tragedy, as a means
of protest and in service of those in need. Music is a central feature of Terlinguan social life and an expression of the
collective identity of its residents. "Out in West Texas, a
hundred miles from nowhere," as one local songwriter puts
it, Terlingua musicians daily defy the conventional narrative suggesting that only certain people are inherently musical, or that densely populated urban areas are necessarily
the epicenters for music in the United States. In challenging
these established ideas, Terlinguans have created a distinct
musical environment all their own, a scene and a sound that

embody their town and the cherished community spirit that animates it.

I STUMBLED UPON Terlingua's exceptional music scene almost by accident. A doctoral student in ethnomusicology (the study of music from a social and cultural perspective), I had recently begun searching for somewhere in Texas to pursue music research. A Texan by birth, I was tired of hearing most conversations about my home state's rich musical history confined to a few high-profile cities like Austin, Houston, and San Antonio. Having long been interested in the musical lives of "ordinary" people, I thought that the Big Bend region—quirky and off the beaten path as it was—might be an intriguing place to look.

I made a weeklong trip to the Big Bend in spring 2013, intent on exploring some of the region's larger towns in hopes that I might find something compelling to write about. I scoped out Alpine, a college town of six thousand people and the largest settlement in the region. I also checked out Marfa, a town of about seventeen hundred that in recent decades has developed an international reputation for visual art. By prioritizing these places, I was operating on conventional wisdom about what music towns tend to look like; put simply, I assumed, as most people might, that a college town and a village full of artists would be the likeliest places in the region to have reasonably active music scenes. At the time, Terlingua was nowhere on my radar. I knew that Jerry Jeff Walker had recorded a famous Texas country music album in 1973 called ¡Viva Terlingua!, but that it was actually recorded in Luckenbach, Texas, and only earned its name because there happened to be a Terlingua bumper sticker on the door featured on the album cover. I also knew that a chili cook-off was held in the Terlingua area every fall, supposedly one of the largest and longest running in the world. I had no idea that anyone, much less a bunch of musicians, even *lived* in Terlingua during the rest of the year.

I ended up making a last-minute drive to Terlingua after someone in Alpine tipped me off about the Porch. At first, I was skeptical—this dusty outpost in the basement of the country certainly didn't *look* like a music town, at least not as I had always envisioned them. The Porch was mostly empty when I arrived late on a weekday morning, so I grabbed my guitar out of the back of the car and took a seat on one of the benches. The summer heat was still a month or more away, and the coolness radiating from the thick adobe wall at my back sent a slight chill down my spine. I sat forward and looked out at the Chisos Mountains. I couldn't have realized it at the time, but I was about to have my first musical experience in Terlingua, and I would be the one called on to perform.

In perhaps any other setting, Jim Keaveny would stick out like a sore thumb, but on the Terlingua Porch he seems a perfect fit. When he pulled up in his pickup truck, he was wearing a plain white tank top, jean shorts cut off raggedly several inches above the knee, and a pair of dusty flip-flops revealing desert-calloused feet. Around his waist was a brown leather belt that appeared to be homemade, with a buckle fashioned out of a generous slice of deer antler. On his head was a wide-brimmed straw hat that was heavily frayed and warped like a sheet of paper that had been repeatedly soaked and left to dry in the sun. He had long hair, a deep tan, and appeared to be in his early forties. He looked as much a part of the Porch as the benches themselves.

"So, you got a song?" Jim asked as he took a seat on the bench to my right. He pointed to my guitar, which was still lying in its case near my feet. I tuned it up and proceeded to play a pair of covers by well-known Texas singer-songwriters, trying my best to conceal my stage fright as it would seem out of place in such a relaxed setting. Jim listened intently and sang along on both choruses.

"Mind if I borrow that thing?" he asked when I had finished. He pulled out a harmonica and snapped it into playing position in one of those neck cradles that Bob Dylan used to use. I handed him my guitar and he began to sing:

Well my woman dreams in the yard while I dream in the
house
Mom says I eat like a bird and she eats like a mouse
They tell us we're babies but we think that we're gettin'
old
Yippee-i yippee-i yippee-i yippee-ay-oh

Well I got me somethin', and it never cost me much,
don't-cha know
We sleep in each morning until the sun makes it all glow
Sometimes I'll get work, but it never pay much, but it
pay
Yippee-i yippee-i yippee-i yippee-i-ay

Yippee-i yippee-i yippee-i yippee-i-ay
Yippee-i yippee-i yippee-i-oh, so they say
Yippee-i yippee-i yippee-i yippee-i-ay
Yippee-i yippee-i yippee-i-oh everyday

Well my old friends say this ain't no place to find no H2O
Now we ain't had none in a year, but last winter there was
snow
I guess they call it what they call it for a reason, you
know
Ah, but yippee-i yippee-i yippee-i yippee-i-oh

It don't look like much, but I know that progress has been
made
As we wander around each day, always searching for the
shade
Sometimes she'll get blue 'til I remind her there's only one
way,
That's just a-yippee-i yippee-i yippee-i yippee-i-ay

Yippee-i yippee-i yippee-i yippee-i-ay
Yippee-i yippee-i yippee-i-oh, so they say
Yippee-i yippee-i yippee-i yippee-i-ay
Yippee-i yippee-i yippee-i-oh everyday[2]

Some months later, Jim told me that during his youth he would hop trains and ride them across the country, carrying nothing with him but a backpack and a guitar. As he sang, everything about him seemed to conjure this imagery. His strumming style on the guitar was nearer to an attack than a caress; he frailed the strings hard with the backs of his fingernails, embellishing this rhythmic foundation by picking individual notes with enough force that the strings would occasionally slap back and crack against the fretboard. He stomped his foot with such conviction and rhythmic regularity that it became an instrument in itself, essential to and inseparable from the rest of the performance. A road-weary rasp in his voice sounded genuine rather than contrived, and he sang with a vocal delivery that was almost conversational. Taken in sum, his performance exuded such unbridled spirit and vibrancy that I couldn't help but think the trains of his youth must have gained at least as much character from his presence as he did from theirs.

Jim told me that "The Yippee-I-Ay Song" was an original he had written about life in Terlingua. He and his wife had moved to the Big Bend from Austin in 2009. For several years, they had been building a house on Terlingua Ranch, an area of sprawling desert on the north end of South Brewster County. He gave me a tour of his unfinished home the following day. Like most houses in Terlingua, it was simple: a small one-room cabin with a loft for sleeping, a large covered porch facing the massive and breathtaking Nine Point Mesa, and a second covered space in back for an old school bus that served as an addendum to the house. The structure was entirely off-grid, both by choice and by necessity due to its distance from the highway. Like many of their neighbors, they were building on "Terlingua time": do some work and save up a little money, work on the house while the money lasts, then repeat, for months or even years. The house was now far enough along to live in, and Jim was clearly excited about it. They had previously been living in an old caravan trailer while they worked.

"When we came out here, it was tough," Jim remembered. "I mean, we lived in that trailer, that thirteen-foot trailer for four-and-a-half years. Glorified camping is all it was. Oil lamps, coolers, no shade, a little bit of water catchment, but it was a terrible drought, the worst drought they say since 1917. Not a lot of water. We were haulin' water. It was tough." He laughed. "I'm kind of amazed that we made it through that. But we really wanted to be here, that's the thing."

Jim and I continued talking and trading songs for a while longer, and as the morning drifted into afternoon, other vehicles began slowly trickling into the parking lot. During a break between songs, a man wearing sunglasses with purple lenses and a bandana around his head came up to where Jim and I were seated, spotted the guitar, and asked if he could play a song. He reached up and plucked a pick from a crack in the wall (the unofficial Porch pick repository, I later learned), then he lowered himself onto the bench beside me and began to strum and sing.

It's kind of warm here down in Terlingua
And there's lots of little critters that'll sting ya'
Maybe they will, maybe they won't
That's them Terlingua Blues[3]

As the man sang, others in the vicinity started to trickle over to where we were seated, and some even joined in on the refrain. He concluded and passed the guitar to one of these new arrivals, a man with a buoyant expression and a head of enviously thick gray hair that sprung out Medusa-like in all directions. He sat on the ground at the edge of the Porch, his back propped against one of the wooden support beams, and gazed out at the Chisos as he began to strum and sing in a half-spoken proclamatory style.

> It's the heart and soul of a West Texas night
> We'll be singin' till the mornin' light
> Guitars ring, campfires lit
> Just standin' around hip to hip
> Ragtag collection, the greatest hits
> Told our stories, where we went
> I hear heartache, lots of pain
> We could find joy in the pourin' down rain
> Road weary, got the gift of life
> Know when to run, know when to fight
>
> They think we're all crazy. Well, maybe they're right
> But we're the heart and soul of a West Texas night[4]

A chain reaction began: another person took a turn, followed by another and another. Several hours later, the sun was beginning to angle low in the sky when I finally looked up from the circle of performers. There were thirteen people on the Porch and eleven of them had contributed to the music. What's more, I learned that many of the songs I had heard were original compositions, and that a number of them had been recorded at the studio down the road. *Yes,* one of these local songwriters confirmed in response to my obvious incredulity. *Terlingua had its own recording studio.*

I was flabbergasted by what I was witnessing. How many musicians could there possibly be in such an out-of-the-way little town? I returned a few months later to find that my initial experience had not been a fluke. Terlingua was one of the most musically active places I had ever heard of; it was certainly the most musical place I had ever been. Captivated by what I had witnessed, I ended up moving to Terlingua, spending more than two years there between 2013 and 2018, documenting its music, interviewing its residents, and observing and participating in its extraordinary music culture. The book you are holding is the product of that experience.

WHY IS TERLINGUA SO MUSICAL? My first few trips to the Big Bend left me consumed by this question. I wanted to know how Terlingua music began, and whether there was something deeper at play than mere coincidence. Were experienced musicians moving to Terlingua, or did they become steeped in music only after arriving? What percentage of the town's population was musically active? How was it that beginners and advanced musicians were playing together so regularly when this is so rare in the rest of the country? What kinds of music were prevalent in Terlingua? How was the local scene shaped by the town's proximity to the US-Mexico border? Was there any money to be made from music in such a small town? Finally, how might a more complete understanding of musical life in this improbable community change my own preconceptions about music, music towns, and even the nature of human musicality itself?[5]

During my two-plus years living in the lower Big Bend, I made more music with a wider variety of people than at any other period in my life. Moreover, as my familiarity with the place grew, I began to appreciate that Terlingua music and Terlingua life as a whole are inextricably intertwined. Each new insight I gained about local music also led me to deeper, more meaningful insights about the town and its people. I learned that formal gigs and casual Porch jams were more than just two different kinds of musical performance, that they had long histories in Terlingua that imbued them with layers of symbolic meaning for local residents. I realized that the uncanny number of musicians living in Terlingua is no accident—indeed, the town's extraordinary musical atmosphere exists in large part *because* of its small size and remote location, not despite them. I learned that a new class of professional musician is being attracted to Terlingua for reasons that make both creative and financial sense, a trend that upends decades of conventional wisdom about urban areas and their stranglehold on the professional music economy in the United States. I learned that, despite its emphasis on community, a closer look at Terlingua's music scene reveals hidden fractures—widely recognized but rarely spoken about openly—in the social fabric of what is otherwise an extremely close-knit town. I learned that Terlingua is undergoing a period of profound transformation, complete with a growing population and developing infrastructure, and that many residents are concerned that these changes will fundamentally alter the social and musical life of their town. Finally, whenever I heard someone remark that "music just doesn't happen on the Porch like it used to," I began to hear this for what it truly was: a far-reaching comment on Terlingua's history, its cherished social life, and the implications of the town's continued growth—all summed up neatly in a single phrase.

My research continued to evolve as the months progressed, and before long, it had become much more than a simple nuts-and-bolts account of small-town music. In order to properly explain what Porch jams mean to local residents, I would need to trace them back in time to the campfires that gave birth to the Terlingua music scene. An accurate description of amateur music would require a broader description of Terlingua's small-town sense of community. I could not write about the burgeoning professional music economy in Terlingua without addressing the Austin scene to which it is intimately connected. Nor could I discuss Terlingua's status as a border town without first examining earlier decades when the border in the Big Bend was extremely fluid.

Most importantly, I knew that I would never be able to explain to readers why anyone outside Terlingua should care about music in this tiny desert town unless I also contrasted Terlingua's musical life with American musical life more broadly. Research and personal experience had taught me that innate human musicality has largely been stifled in this country for much of the past century, to the point that most Americans no longer believe themselves to possess any fundamental musical ability. This I understood, but I did not fully appreciate its ramifications until I arrived in the Big Bend. Living in Terlingua, where music was more prevalent than anywhere I had ever been, gave me a vision of what might be possible if Americans were encouraged to rethink the role of music in their daily lives. Terlingua is an uncommonly musical town, but its residents are no more genetically predisposed toward music than are the residents of any other town. Terlingua is musical because Terlinguans have *chosen* music. That choice is what I wanted to understand most of all.

During my time in the Big Bend, I often recalled a quote by the influential British ethnomusicologist John Blacking. Music, he said, "is a metaphorical expression of feelings associated with the way society really is."[6] I agree, but I would go one step further: music is also an expression of the way society *strives* to be. When we pour ourselves into the music we create, we lay bare our aspirations and our realities alike, revealing ourselves both as we wish to be and as we really are. Such is the power of music, that most universal and human of art forms—it is a sonic embodiment of our truest selves.

In Terlingua, music is many things. It is a record of the town's history and a profession of hope for its future. It is a celebration of what makes Terlingua life special and an appeal for preserving that life for future generations. It is a representation of Terlingua in all its glory and imperfection, a space where ideals are negotiated and identity is asserted. It is the soul of Terlingua expressed in sound.

On the Porch is a musical biography of a tiny but remarkable town. In telling the unlikely story of music in Terlingua, it provides an intimate look into the collective experiences of the people who create that music—their values, their shared history, the ups and downs that shape their lives, their fears and hopes for the future. Above all, *On the Porch* is a celebration of human musicality, of the role that music plays and can play in our lives, both in Terlingua and beyond.

That's them Terlingua Blues.

CHAPTER I

STARLIGHT AND STAGE LIGHTS

WHEN YOU CROSS THE THRESHOLD from the Porch into
the Starlight Theatre, it is immediately apparent that you are
entering a fundamentally different kind of space. The Porch
is the epitome of informal, a hangout rather than a place of
business. With its crumbling adobe walls, its tin cans repur-
posed as ashtrays, the wind-worn guitars and washtub bass
propped in the corner, and even the occasional horse hitched
to its support beams, it looks like the setting for a classic
Western. Constructed around 1908 and scarcely renovated
since that time, it would almost seem like an anachronism
were it not located in such an out-of-the-way part of the
world. The music that takes place on the Porch only serves
to reinforce this image. It never occurs on a predetermined
day or at a prearranged time, but rather arises organically.
Participation does not require an invitation, and personnel
are in constant flux. Musicians freely come and go as they
please, joining the performance or not as suits their individual desires. The Porch has no stage, no space set aside for
musicians to inhabit. When music does occur, it shares real
estate with whatever else might be taking place that day.
Aside from the occasional unsolicited gratuity deposited in
an open instrument case, musicians are not compensated
monetarily. They play for their own entertainment, not for
an audience.

The Starlight Theatre possesses a different character entirely. It is the closest thing that West Texas has to a European cathedral in the sense that it seems to exist in both the past and present simultaneously. Constructed in 1936 as a movie theater for the mining residents of early Terlingua, it was abandoned in the 1940s along with the rest of the town and gradually fell into disrepair. A half-century later, the building was resurrected, and today it is a bustling restaurant and bar, among the largest employers and most successful businesses in all of South Brewster County.

While the Porch's appearance misleadingly suggests that it has been neglected rather than cherished over the years, the Starlight gives the impression that it has been carefully manicured. One of the first things that many people notice upon entering the Starlight is the interior walls: true to their Ghost Town roots, they have been retained in their slowly deteriorating state, reminding patrons that they are dining in a reclaimed adobe ruin. Heavy footfalls reveal that a false floor was added at some point, constructed on top of the original sloping floor. Like the pieces of the building itself, the decorations adorning the interior have been added bit-by-bit over time and are by turns weird or kitschy in a Disney World sort of way or totally captivating in their singularity. Sun-bleached animal skulls hang from the rafters, and faux human skeletons—a prevailing motif in the Terlingua Ghost Town—are made to look as if they have been partially imbedded in the walls. A portrait of Pancho Villa hangs above the bar. On a side wall, a local artist resourcefully used several exposed layers of crumbling plaster to paint a stunning reproduction of a colorful Chisos sunset. At the far end of the room is a large concrete dance floor where photographs, paintings, and sculptures by a rotating cast of Terlingua artists form a makeshift gallery. Perched on a pedestal nearby is a large stuffed male goat, impressively horned, with an upturned bottle of Lone Star beer in his mouth. This is Clay Henry, the once honorary mayor in these parts.

Terlingua musicians perform on the Starlight Theatre's main stage, 2014.

The focal point of the Starlight's interior is the main stage. Between the sound booth, the array of monitors, the stacks of speakers, and the microphones and microphone stands, it is obvious to even the most casual observer that the approach to music in this room is categorically different. While the Porch is a space for jams, the Starlight is a venue for gigs. As such, it does not provide the same open platform for participation as the Porch—on the contrary, you have to be invited to play here. The Starlight is a business, after all, where live music is booked for the entertainment of paying customers. A barrier for entry is to be expected.

The most memorable feature of the interior is the striking floor-to-ceiling mural that serves as a backdrop for the main stage. Highly detailed and clearly the work of a skilled hand, the mural depicts a dozen or so miners or cowboys, mostly Mexican, gathered around a campfire amid the dilapidated ruins. Some are drinking coffee, some are smoking pipes, and one is strumming a guitar. Behind them is a picture-perfect representation of the Chisos Mountains at night. The only sources of light are the campfire and the brilliant starry sky. It is an image of the Terlingua Ghost Town as it once was— or rather, as it is imagined to have been—during some unspecified moment in the past.

Although they are directly adjacent to one another—exit the one and you've entered the other—the Porch and the Starlight are such qualitatively different spaces that even the local dogs have learned to recognize the distinction, roaming freely on the Porch but stopping in their tracks the moment they reach the Starlight's front door. The two places weren't always so different, however. Before the Starlight became a business, it too was a dilapidated hangout, a place where the early inhabitants of reborn Terlingua would gather to socialize beneath the clear desert sky. The Starlight earned its name in those days when the adobe ruin had no roof to obscure the heavens. The bar wasn't there back then. Neither was the kitchen nor the new level floor. Behind the stage was another mural, older than the one currently on display. Roughly sketched in chalk, it depicted eleven people standing side by side in front of a mountainous desert sunset. Enter the Starlight today and you will find no sign of this mural; I only learned of its existence through word of mouth. But it is immediately clear, when viewing photographs of the older mural, that these were real people. They have beards and bangs, long hair and short hair. Some are holding beers, and a few have their hands in their pockets, but most have their arms around the people to their left and right. It is a depiction of Terlingua in the early years of its rebirth.[1]

I have been in the Starlight Theatre more times than I can count, and I have heard many stories of the building's history from people who were present in the opening years of the Terlingua renaissance. Enough remains of the original structure that it is easy to imagine this building as it once was: before the roof was added, when there were no lights or rafters to obscure the stars; before the floor was built, when the rain would come down and collect in pools at the base of the stage, providing refuge for frogs and tadpoles; before the electricity was installed, when a gaggle of river guides, perhaps smelly from days of rafting and irregular bathing, would hold potlucks under the moonlight, singing and dancing and strumming guitars the way they still do on the Porch—not for an audience, but for each other. Standing in this room today must be a poignant experience for those who remain, that handful of veterans from the earliest days of Terlingua's rebirth who have stuck around to see Terlingua as it exists in the twenty-first century. I wonder if they cross the threshold into the Starlight and glimpse those familiar crumbling walls, then peer out over the sea of diners to the newer, more sightly mural behind the stage, and remember.

Like a phoenix, Terlingua was reborn out of crumbling ruins in the late 1970s, and in a way, the town's entire history in the decades since is embodied by the relationship between the Starlight and the Porch. Two of the oldest structures in the lower Big Bend, they have been among the most important gathering places in the region since the moments they were built. Today they form Terlingua's social and musical nucleus: I played more gigs at one, and more jams at the other, than at any other place during the two years I lived in Terlingua. Their physical proximity, however, only serves to highlight the divergent histories of these two spaces. One polished and commercial, the other battered and egalitarian, they have come to symbolize two poles of the Terlingua experience, two extremes in a long line of changes that many local residents still struggle to reconcile. In these spaces, and in their music, lies much of Terlingua's story.

FROM CAMPFIRES TO PORCH JAMS

During the first half of the twentieth century, Terlingua, Texas, was synonymous with mercury mining. The Chisos

Mining Company, the largest mining operation in the Big Bend, was responsible for constructing what today is known as the Terlingua Ghost Town, and for decades virtually all of the town's residents were either employees of the company or their families.[2] When the global market for mercury crashed in the years following World War II, the mines of Terlingua closed for good, and with no other reason to remain, most residents moved away. For thirty years the abandoned town was largely ignored, treated as little more than a passing curiosity off a lonely highway. In 1967, the Ghost Town again gained a measure of notoriety when the Porch served as the location for a now legendary chili cook-off between Texan Wick Fowler and New Yorker H. Allen Smith. What was envisioned as a one-off contest has since become a pair of annual events that bring thousands of visitors to Terlingua every fall. Indeed, most people who have heard of Terlingua only know of its existence because of these cook-offs.[3] For the rest of the year, however, Terlingua remained all but forgotten.

The Terlingua Ghost Town was still mostly deserted when two young river guides named Mike Davidson and Steve Harris moved there in spring 1977. Their new company, Far Flung Adventures, had just received a permit to operate commercial rafting trips on the Big Bend section of the Rio Grande, a stretch of river with some three hundred miles of canyon country that until then had been little explored by commercial ventures. The partners were on their own when they arrived. Other than a smattering of ranchers, some national park employees (who lived almost exclusively within the park), and a handful of other residents, the whole of South Brewster County was empty. "When we moved here we increased the population of the Ghost Town by 200 percent, from one to three," said Davidson with a chuckle. The partners set up shop in the abandoned Chisos Company Store at the opposite end of the Porch from the Starlight. Paying a modest rent to the Ghost Town's owner, they converted the ruin into their company headquarters and opened their doors for business. During its first year of operation, Far Flung's only two employees were its founders. Then, in a stroke of fortune for the young river guides, a 1979 article in *Southern Living* featured a profile of the company, and by spring 1980, Far Flung had grown to a dozen employees. Like Harris and Davidson before them, most of these early residents moved directly into the Ghost Town, choosing from among the rock and adobe ruins to find those that could be made habitable once again. Suddenly, Terlingua was back in business, this time with a pair of river rats at the helm.

Far Flung Adventures was a simple operation during its first few decades, with the Porch serving as its de facto front lobby. "Terlingua was a river town," recalled fiddler Mark Lewis, who moved to Terlingua in 1990 to work for the company. "Back then, it was all about Far Flung Adventures. Everyone who lived in town worked for Far Flung. And the trips came and went from the Porch. Guides jumped out of the van, opened the doors for the customers, collected a tip and came up on the Porch and bought everybody a beer, and that was who was on the Porch. There was hardly anybody livin' around here. You could camp anywhere."

As isolated as Terlingua feels today, it pales in comparison to the reborn town's first few decades. The nearest potable water in those days was at Panther Junction in the national park, a sixty-mile round-trip from the Ghost Town. Electricity was spotty at best, and many residents lived without it entirely. There was no plumbing of any kind. The Study Butte Store near the national park entrance carried a limited supply of canned goods and other mostly nonperishable items, and the closest reliable source of produce was a rowboat ride across the Rio Grande in Paso Lajitas—a relatively easy twenty-five-mile round-trip in those days when the border in the region was still fluid. There was no television, no internet, and other than a faint AM broadcast from Chihuahua City that you could sometimes pick up on hilltops, there was no radio. People gathered every evening around campfires rather than in restaurants and bars.

While this glorified camping might sound like an undue amount of hardship for people living in a developed nation in the late twentieth century, longtime Terlingua residents remember those early years fondly. With very few people in town, those who were present felt a strong sense of solidarity with one another, united as they were by a common goal in that unlikely place: *row the river, live simply, repeat*. A deep appreciation for the landscape was made all the more real by their work, by the ramshackle conditions in which they lived, and by the absence of air conditioning and other amenities that would buffer them from constant exposure to the natural world. You had two choices in those days: embrace the desert or get the hell out.

It is easier to appreciate what lured those first intrepid river guides to early Terlingua when you've witnessed the Big Bend for yourself. The Apaches who once lived in the area believed that the lower Big Bend was formed haphazardly when the Creator found an empty place to discard all the rubble that remained after making the Earth.[4] One look at the region reveals why this belief took root. If the iconic American mountain ranges—the Rockies, the Cascades, the High Sierra—are the Mona Lisas of mountains, uniform and perfectly proportioned, the lower Big Bend is the modern artist's canvas onto which projectile paint has been erratically flung. Hoodoos and other ghostly outcroppings jut skyward in singles and clusters. Seemingly random outcroppings of jumbled rocks, jarring and angled as if charged with electricity, lie strewn atop formations that flow like layers of petrified cake batter. Individual mountains, standing like sentinels in their isolation, alternate with cloistered miniranges. Mesas of all different heights and breadths—some no larger than a house, some so vast you can stand on them without realizing you are on a mesa at all—provide contrast

Big Bend National Park, 2013.

against the sharper contours of nearby jagged peaks. Walls of rock thousands of feet high tower above the desert lowlands, so neatly formed that they would almost appear man-made if not for their immense scale. Cut into these natural barriers are steep-walled canyons, curiosities in that they are approached from water level rather than from the rim. The vast open spaces that connect these myriad features appear flat, but they are often tilted in one direction or another so that the bases of mountains are offset, sometimes by thousands of feet, making it impossible to discern the true size of each feature compared to every other. Distance becomes an optical illusion: plains that stretch for miles are compressed to inches by the eye. The air is often so clear, the humidity so low, that on the very best days a person can read the contours of mountains a hundred miles away like the pages of a book. Overlay all this incongruous geology with the region's equally distinctive flora and fauna and it is little wonder why the early residents of reborn Terlingua, living in happy squalor at the margins of American society, fell so quickly and so completely in love. They looked at the land and saw themselves.

Situated as they were in this isolated environment, Terlingua residents originally began making music out of necessity. With few other options for entertainment, river guides made music every night after the sun went down. "Back in those days we had to make our own fun," recalled Davidson. "One of the common questions from our customers was, 'What do you *do* down here?' Well, one of the things we did was make music, just jammin' on the river and by campfires and stuff like that. It wasn't in a commercial place 'cause there wasn't one. Instead, there would be a campfire somewhere, and you'd bring your bedroll and your drinks and everyone would come out and jam. That was the first musical expression here in the Terlingua Ghost Town."

Campfire jams remained at the heart of Terlingua life for decades, and their importance for the town's early residents would be difficult to overstate. "The campfires *defined* the community," said Ted Arbogast, who moved to Terlingua in the mid-1990s. "You'd have musicians play, and the people who weren't musicians were maybe tendin' to the barbeque. Songs would get passed around that were all about the people and the chemistry that was this place."

There is something ancient and deeply human about these stories of campfires in early Terlingua. Campfires have played a critical role in human social life ever since our hominid ancestors first developed the ability to create fire more than a million years ago. According to anthropologist Polly Wiessner, fire's efficacy in the pre-industrialized world extended far beyond its ability to provide warmth or cook food. Perhaps even more significantly, firelight effectively extended daytime, providing additional hours of light and a centralized space in which to be socially active.[5] Moreover, because standard daytime activities such as procuring food and water were impossible within the limited confines of the firelight, people were instead free to use this additional time for non-subsistence activities, including storytelling, religious rituals, and music making. Indeed, since the control of fire preceded these and other cultural institutions in human history, it is not out of the question to suggest that many of the most significant features that define the human experience—music, language, and religion, among them—developed in large part thanks to the qualitatively different kinds of social spaces that campfires created.

Today, campfires have lost much of their significance in the developed world. No longer the primary means for providing food, heat, light, and safety, fires have also relinquished their role as centers of social and cultural life. Camping trips and music festivals preserve this tradition to a limited degree, and anyone who has ever sat around a fire in such a setting can likely testify to the campfire's social utility. But these events represent special occasions, not norms of everyday life for most people. In the first few decades of Terlingua's rebirth, however—when the population was small, electricity was scarce, and few other forms of entertainment existed—campfires remained the primary centers for social life well into the 1990s. These were the bars, the community centers, the living rooms of early Terlingua. Ultimately, campfires also helped to highlight Terlingua's essential differentness, functioning alongside eastern sunsets and idiosyncratic landscapes to further distinguish the town as a place all its own.

Although campfires were the heart and soul of early Terlingua, they were not the only informal music spaces in town. There was the Study Butte Store, a small grocery near the entrance to Big Bend National Park, where groups of local musicians would gather daily during the 1980s and early 90s to sit in the shade, drink beer, and jam. There was also the Lajitas Trading Post, located on the Rio Grande about twelve miles southwest of the Ghost Town. For much of the twentieth century, the Trading Post was a major social and economic hub for an enormous swath of sparsely populated desert on both sides of the river. Residents of small towns in the Mexican states of Chihuahua and Coahuila, isolated by long drives over rough roads from the larger cities to the south, would cross the international boundary at Lajitas to buy staple foods and gasoline, often stopping to sing or play some music before heading back home across the river.

Last but not least, there was the Porch, today the most frequented spot in the lower Big Bend for informal jams. Terlingua residents have described the Porch variously as "Terlingua's clubhouse," "the lifeblood of this place," "the center of our community," and "like a church, where lots of different people with different personalities come together." It is little wonder that it has also become such a popular place for music.

Porch music differs markedly from the onstage performances more common in developed nations like the United States. This is not a question of "genre" or "style," but rather a question of whom the music is intended to please. Porch jams, like the campfire jams that preceded them, are informal musical events intended primarily for the enjoyment of the participants themselves.[6] Because jamming musicians are freed from the burden of entertaining an audience, the music they create often looks and sounds completely different from what one would hear in a typical onstage performance. Most jams are open to a wide array of performers, and some, like those on the Porch, are open to anyone who wants to join regardless of ability level or previous musical experience. Porch jams are decidedly informal; there is plenty of room for looseness and experimentation, for talking to each other between and even during songs, for working through new material, for learning new songs on the fly. Jams have a magical air of spontaneity about them, a feeling that anything can happen because nothing is planned.[7]

Unlike some of the more structured jams that I have witnessed in other parts of the country, Porch jams are wholly

Sunday afternoon jam on the Terlingua Porch, 2018.

spontaneous. They can happen any day and at any time: you might show up for several days in a row without hearing a thing, or you might get lucky and witness a jam that grows to include twenty or more participants. I learned to always be prepared, carrying at least a guitar with me at all times whether I was expecting music or not.

"I've never seen anything else like the Porch," said Terlingua resident Jim Keaveny, who has toured extensively as a singer-songwriter throughout Europe and North America. "It's a special place that can take off or not take off. Sometimes the Porch just goes crazy in a big ol' jam, but you *definitely* can't hold your breath. It could be the sleepiest place in the world or it could be completely off the hook. It might start with one or two people playin', and then others start comin' around, and next thing you know there's a five- or six-piece band."

Terlingua fiddler Anna Oakley agreed. "We have a friend from Kerrville who is a great musician, and we told him,

'You gotta come hang out on the Porch and we'll play music.' And then he showed up and he goes, 'When does the music start?' And we were like, 'Well . . . you kinda have to be the one to start it.' You never know, it could be totally dead or it could be a day when the whole Porch is involved."

A defining feature of Porch music is that it is entirely non-commercial, meaning that payment is neither offered to nor expected by participating musicians. This is something of a rarity in capitalist countries like the United States, where the overwhelming majority of music is monetized in some way, directly or indirectly. Sometimes visitors to Terlingua, likely unaccustomed to seeing such jams, will drop money into an open guitar case as they might for a busker on the street. However, this action betrays a lack of awareness of the difference between buskers—who are essentially performing for an audience on the street rather than from the stage—and Porch musicians, who would still be playing even if there was no one around to hear them. In fact, the Porch is such a staunchly *anti*-commercial venue that musicians who try to promote themselves over their fellow participants sometimes become the targets of a de facto boycott. Occasionally, someone new to town will show up to a Porch jam peddling their CDs, or will plug into an amplifier as they would for an audience, or will do something else that signals they do not fully appreciate that the Porch is an intentional alternative to the stage. Almost invariably, these offenders are given the cold shoulder until they either leave or realize the error of their behavior.

I must admit that I have developed a certain fondness for Porch jams. Having spent a good portion of my life formally training to perform music professionally onstage, I found something rapturous and refreshing about moving to Terlingua and jamming on the Porch every day. It reminded me of the annual camping trips our family took when I was a kid, when we would sit around a campfire at night and listen while a few people passed a guitar back and forth and everyone else happily sang along. Jamming on the Porch, I felt transported to those campfires, to those indelible moments in my formative years when music wasn't about striving for perfection or appealing to an audience, but was simply about the joy of sharing the experience with the people around you. These were moments when it didn't matter how the music sounded—it only mattered how the music felt. Moving to Terlingua re-grounded me as a musician. Jams like these, I realized, were the reason I fell in love with music in the first place.

The spontaneous and meandering nature of Porch jams is impossible to capture fully on camera or in recordings. Because they lack set starting and ending times, Porch jams tend to be spread throughout the day—sometimes spanning ten hours or more—with musicians drifting constantly between playing music and chatting with their friends. A five-minute video clip can show you a single song, but it cannot capture a Porch jam's essence. It won't reveal how music is but a single thread—albeit an important one—in a much larger social tapestry, one that is constantly interwoven with talking and dancing and countless other forms of communication, connecting both musicians and non-musicians alike.

I am often asked what genre of music is performed in Terlingua. Although singer-songwriter music in the Austin tradition (acoustic folk, progressive country, Americana) is the predominant style of music in town, the truest answer to this question is that it depends on who is playing at the time. I recall a particularly good day of Porch music that occurred in early February a few years after I moved to the Big Bend. I had arrived early at the Starlight to record a brunch performance by Terlingua Tanz, a quartet of local musicians who play a wide variety of classically inspired international dance music. A Porch jam began around two o'clock when a few members of the quartet, having concluded their gig in the Starlight, moved outside to continue the music. Playing as a duet with accordion and classical guitar, they began singing "Ridin' Down the Canyon," an old Gene Autry song. "We're really showing our age with this one!" Charlie, the accordion player, joked between verses. The duo played a few more classic country songs before a bearded musician in his early twenties arrived with his guitar and led the group—now a trio—in several heavy alt-rock numbers. Someone requested an encore performance of a tango that Terlingua Tanz had played during their gig, and a few couples stood up from the benches to dance as the musicians obliged. A bit later, a part-time local musician arrived at the Porch with his guitarrón (a large-bodied bass guitar commonly used in Mexican mariachi music), and he proceeded to lead the group in renditions of two Spanish-language songs, the well-known Mexican song "Cielito Lindo" followed by the classic Puerto Rican bolero "En Mi Viejo San Juan."

The jam went on more or less uninterrupted as additional musicians continued to congregate. One of these new arrivals, a Dobro player who was visiting from out of town, began playing some bluesy licks while most of the other musicians were lost in conversation. Tim, the classical guitarist from Terlingua Tanz, started playing accompaniment behind the Dobro, and soon other instruments joined the fray, including the guitarrón, a jaw harp, and an udu (a clay pot-shaped percussion instrument of Igbo [Nigerian] origin). As the impromptu blues jam continued to gain momentum, Tim began improvising lyrics:

> Well, if I was in Louisiana
> I think I might have the blues
> Well, if I was in Louisiana
> I think I just might have the blues
> But I'm here in Terlingua
> Wearin' my cowboy shoes
>
> I'm happy, happy, happy
> I'm hap-happy, happy, happy . . .

Well, if I was back in Ohio
With six inches of snow
I'd have me a nice fire
And my woman in an afterglow
But if I was in Louisiana
I think I'd have the blues

While Tim was singing, a local resident named Jamie, who was sitting on the nearest bench, turned away from the conversation next to him and began paying closer attention to the performance. As Tim ended his third verse, Jamie leaned into the circle of musicians and, without warning, began singing his own new verses to the song:

Cause it's two feet of snow up on the ground
But not here in the desert where I'm found
We go out on the Porch
Try to find the souls in each and every sort
I don't know exactly where I'm goin'
But joyride along the way

This was a first. Never before had I seen Jamie participate in local music (he later confirmed to me that this had been the first time in his life he had ever sung in public). The blues continued with the two singers now alternating, playing off each other while the instrumentalists backed them up:

Tim:
Hey Terlingua
Hey Terlingua
We love you here
We like the beer
Heyyy-o

Jamie:
We love the beer, there ain't cops near

We can be whatever we want with no fear
Be who you wanna be
Run around naked, it don't bother me
Dance around doin' that tango, too
Sittin' around and drink more than I do, but
We do it in Terlingua

Tim:
(Hey Terlingua)

Jamie:
Well, we do it in Terlingua, yeah

Tim:
(Hey Terlingua)

Jamie:
We do what we do, we do what we can
Try to walk tall, hold our head like a man, ohhhhh . . .

The instrumentalists went around the circle now, taking turns improvising short solos before the vocalists entered a final time to conclude the song:

Tim:
In Terlingua
It's good to be here
Enjoying a cold beer
It's the best place on Earth

Jamie:
Terlingua . . .

The Porch jam continued until the sun had set and the guitarists could no longer see their fingers on the strings. As the final few musicians packed up their instruments, I glanced at my watch: there had been almost nine hours of continuous music on the Porch with close to twenty

Musicians on the Terlingua Porch, 2018.

different people contributing. This would have been an un-paralleled musical experience during any other period of my life. It was just another Sunday Funday in Terlingua.

Informal jams were the first musical events that took place in reborn Terlingua. In those early years, when the local population was only a few dozen strong and campfires were among the only places to socialize, jams meshed perfectly with the relaxed pace and casual spirit of Terlingua life. Today, such jams still happen almost every day, and they have become one of the highlights of the Terlingua experience for both locals and visitors. Residents are well aware that the jamming atmosphere in their town has few parallels elsewhere in the United States, and for this reason, Porch jams have become yet another source of pride for many of the people who call Terlingua home. Like eastern sunsets, they are a symbol of what makes Terlingua unique. *In Terlingua, we do things a little differently.*

THE BIRTH OF COMMERCIAL SPACES

The Terlingua music scene might be rooted in Porch and campfire jams, but these are far from the only musical events in town. In fact, commercial gigs in one form or another date back to the earliest years of Terlingua's rebirth. At Far Flung Adventures, what began modestly as river guides packing guitars to entertain themselves in camp soon grew into the Texas River Music Series, a dedicated series of music rafting trips that began in the early 1980s and still takes place today. Marketed by Far Flung as one-of-a-kind package deals combining rafting trips with concerts, each trip is organized with a particular musician in mind—usually a well-known Texas songwriter—and fans from across the state or country travel to Terlingua for the opportunity to join a renowned musician on a float down the Rio Grande capped by an intimate performance in camp.[8] They are essentially house concerts on the river, and they were among the first paid musical performances in South Brewster County. Two of the earliest featured performers, the acclaimed Texas songwriters Steve Fromholz and Butch Hancock, eventually moved to Terlingua and became Far Flung boatmen themselves.

During the 1990s, when the Rio Grande still ran high enough for consistent rafting (these days most trips take place in canoes), Far Flung also offered gourmet river trips, where clients were treated each night to live music and multi-course meals prepared by a trained chef. "Sometimes they even brought classical quartets down there," recalled musician and retired Far Flung boatman Laird Considine. "Yeah, people went down there with their *cellos* and stuff!"

Laird participated in a number of Far Flung's music trips, both as a musician and as a boatman, and it was obvious that the experience had a profound effect on him. "You would not *believe* what it's like to be at one of those camps inside Santa Elena Canyon," he told me over beers one evening. "You go down into the canyon to where you've only got this small sliver of sky above you, and the canyon walls are like 1,200 feet on either side of the river. And then it gets dark, so that you've got this river of stars above you that mirrors the river of water. Then the moon starts shining down and reflecting off the walls, and all the rocks start changing their shapes, and the shadows change. And the *sound* in there . . ." Laird paused, a look of reverence overtaking his face. "The sound in that canyon, Chase. You strum a guitar and you can hear it go *whoo . . . ooo . . . ooo . . . ooo . . . .* And that's just an acoustic guitar. Imagine what your saxophone would do in there. With the acoustics bouncing off the water and the rocks and everything, the saxophone would just be so . . . I tell you what, I'd row a freakin' boat to hear that."

In addition to riverside gigs, interest in creating more formalized bands also dates back to those early years. The first local band, the Terlingua All-Stars, was created in 1980, only three years after Far Flung Adventures was founded. According to Mike Davidson—a founding member of the band as well as the rafting company—the impetus for the All-Stars arose partially out of frustration with the inherent limitations of the local campfire music scene. "We literally flipped," he recalled. "We were always doing these little campfire jams, and we had this guy who would come and play saxophone, but he wasn't very good at it and it was real overpowering. So we decided we needed to get a band, you know, so that we could turn the volume up and not hear this other guy. We had a banjo, a bass, drums, trombone, and a lead singer, and we ended up playing a lot of reggae and rhythm and blues."

It was difficult at first for the Terlingua All-Stars to find places to play since there were no real venues in South Brewster County at that time. Some of their earliest performances took place in the Starlight Theatre—still roofless— when they ran an extension cord over the adobe wall from a gas generator outside to power their amps and microphones. The handful of Terlingua residents who are still around to remember those years recall these performances fondly, when they danced with their fellow raft guides under the brilliant banner of the sky. The first true commercial venue in South Brewster County arrived one year later, when La Kiva Restaurant & Bar opened for business in 1981. The owner, Gil Felts, was a music lover and an enthusiastic supporter of local artists, and many Terlingua musicians recall scoring their first-ever paying gigs at La Kiva.

As Far Flung's operation grew, so did the population of the town, and soon other venues followed in La Kiva's footsteps. Uncle Joe's Café and the Boatman's Bar & Grill were both about five miles down the road from the Ghost Town in Study Butte, and The Longhorn was twenty miles or so north on Highway 118 near Terlingua Ranch. Pam Ware's Desert Deli Diner and the Ghost Town Saloon were both in the Ghost Town, a short walk from the Porch and the Starlight. Partially in response to these new performance opportunities—but also because the number of local musicians had grown—more Terlingua musicians began coalescing into formally organized bands. Following the Terlingua All-Stars were the Craig Carter Band; Charlie Maxwell & Chihuahua, who played country covers and originals; The Rafters, a trio of river guides; Doug Davis & the Note Ropers, who played Texas swing; the Flying Javelinas, a rock 'n' roll power trio; Just Us Girls, an all-female folk band; Los Pinche Gringos, who are still around today and play a combination of classic rock and Mexican cumbia and norteño; the Porch Dawgs, a trio formed on the Study Butte Porch, who played mostly folk music; and Folkadelic, a folk-rock jam band along the lines of the Grateful Dead.

"It was kind of a succession of bands," local songwriter Bryn Moore recalls. "One would be around for a while and then it would morph into something different. But there was not a lot of choice like there is now. There was like one thing to do once or twice a week, so everybody would come 'cause it was the only thing to do."

The gigs that these bands played differed from Porch and campfire jams in some important ways. Because gigs exist for the purpose of entertaining a listening audience, greater emphasis is naturally placed on producing a high-quality musical product. Gigging musicians often rehearse ahead of their performances, whereas rehearsals for a jam are practically unheard of. Participation in gigs is generally by invite only, and in most places it is considered impolite to ask permission to sit in on someone else's show. Not surprisingly, a greater emphasis on quality inevitably leads to more uniformity in the ability levels of the musicians, with more skilled players usually being given more opportunities to perform than less skilled ones.

While jams can and do occur just about anywhere, gigs are typically performed in more standardized settings, often in commercial spaces such as concert halls, nightclubs, theaters, bars, and restaurants. Because this kind of performance is more formal than a jam, it comes with a different standard of etiquette that varies depending on the venue and the style of music being performed. For example, audience members attending a performance at a concert hall or in an intimate listening-focused venue might be expected to remain silent while the music is being played and to clap at certain specified intervals. The performers are also governed by codes of etiquette. A singer-songwriter might be expected to provide intermittent stylized banter between songs in order to keep listeners entertained, while a dance band tries to segue quickly from one song to the next in order to minimize downtime between dances. Though proper behavior varies from style to style, it is always informed by the same primary objective: entertaining the audience.

The gigging scene in Terlingua grew out of campfire jams, and this connection is still palpable in many local performances today. While most Terlingua musicians adhere to some semblance of the above etiquette when they play in commercial venues around town, the approach to gigging

Terlingua musicians perform for diners from the Starlight Theatre's small stage, 2014.

in Terlingua is far more casual than what is typical elsewhere. Rehearsals, for one, are all but nonexistent in Terlingua; I played more than one hundred gigs during my time in town, but I doubt I attended five rehearsals during that span. This relaxed attitude toward gigging is equally apparent in musicians' onstage behavior. I was surprised to find, for example, that very few Terlingua musicians who perform paying gigs make any attempt to dress differently for those performances. During my years as a gigging musician in other parts of the country, I had developed a wardrobe specifically for performing, but when I arrived in Terlingua, I saw musicians wearing sweatpants onstage during some of the busiest nights of the year. During one show at the Starlight, I watched as a band member ate dinner onstage between songs, holding his upright bass with one hand while taking bites of a chicken sandwich with the other. On another occasion, a local band without a predetermined set list spent as much as four to five minutes between songs, talking to each other, making jokes, telling stories, arguing over what song to play, trying to recall songs they had forgotten, talking through the microphone to friends across the room, and even going out to hug said friends. The audience, for their part, was clearly divided about the performance. Some people were obviously put off by the display, while others were having a great time hooping and hollering, yelling back and forth in conversation with the performers, and loudly haggling band members about spending too much time between songs—"Just play the damn song!" someone yelled after the band had made several false starts. To this day, it continues to be the most casual onstage performance I have ever witnessed.

While gigs in Terlingua might be much less formal than their counterparts in other places, this is not to say that Terlingua musicians are unaware of the distinction between gigs and jams. Casual though they are, gigs in Terlingua are ultimately guided by the same basic principles observed everywhere else: namely, a stricter delineation between audience and performer, as well as a greater emphasis on the quality of the product rather than on the inclusiveness of the process. For a town whose musical life began around campfires—an egalitarian musical space if ever one existed—the development of commercial gigs in Terlingua meant that at least some local musicians were beginning to decide that this was a trade-off worth making.

Today, the Terlingua area is home to a half-dozen commercial venues that provide regular gigging opportunities for local musicians, along with a handful of others that do so on special occasions. As of this writing, the Starlight Theatre features live music at least six nights a week, and La Kiva is beginning to approach that number as well. The Thirsty Goat Saloon in Lajitas (twelve miles down the road from the Ghost Town) has live music four or five nights a week, as does the High Sierra Bar & Grill in Terlingua, while the Bad Rabbit Café and Longdraw Pizza feature music mostly on weekends. The Chisos Mountain Lodge in Big Bend National Park hires local acts to perform during their busy periods, and La Posada Milagro, a coffee shop and café next to the Starlight, also features sporadic performances of live music. Recurring hayrides and cookouts offered by the Lajitas Resort provide some Terlingua musicians with additional income for playing around campfires for tourists. Other venues have come and gone: The Longhorn, Ghost Town Saloon, Boatman's Bar & Grill, and Pam Ware's Desert Deli Diner were all memories by the time I arrived in Terlingua. The Boathouse—so named because it was where Far Flung stored their rafts and canoes before being converted into a bar and restaurant—was one of the centers of Terlingua's musical life during my time there, but it too closed its doors in April 2016.

As Terlingua's population climbs and tourist traffic continues to increase, more and more restaurants and bars have opened in order to accommodate this growth, so that today there are more commercial venues than at any other point in the town's history. Over the years, the social scene of South Brewster County has become increasingly concentrated into these commercial spaces, and music making has naturally followed in turn. Campfire jams, once the heart and soul of the town's social and musical life, no longer occur with the regularity they once did, much to the disappointment of many longtime residents. Several of the other major local spaces for jams are also no longer frequented. The Study Butte Store has been deserted for decades, and the old Lajitas Trading Post was purchased by a multimillionaire from Austin and converted into a golf pro shop in the early 2000s. While the Terlingua musical landscape has never been static—both venues and the musicians who frequent them come and go—the town's musical focus seems to have shifted as the population has grown. Most longtime locals recognize that gigs have become the new normal for Terlingua musicians, while jams—including those on the

Porch—are becoming less and less of a daily social activity for many residents.

The most significant change of all came when the Starlight Theatre was converted from an empty ruin into a thriving business. The Starlight had long been an informal hangout for locals. An extension of the campfire scene, it was also a unique social space in its own right. There were potlucks and parties, dances and jams, people passing guitars the same way they did everywhere else in those days. That changed in the early 1990s when the Starlight was leased by Rob and Angie Dean. The couple refurbished the ruin, adding a roof and a new level floor, wiring the building for electricity, and converting the venue into a successful bar and restaurant. It opened for business on New Year's Eve 1991.

The Starlight's transformation was a major event in Terlingua's history. Until this point, the handful of commercial venues that had sprouted up in South County were additions to existing gathering places, not replacements for them. The remaking of the Starlight was the first time that one of Terlingua's non-commercial social spaces was converted into a place of business, the first time that a hangout for jams was replaced by a venue for gigs. Even now, more than thirty years later, many locals who witnessed the change continue to lament the Starlight's transformation, remembering it as a particularly poignant moment in Terlingua's history.

"I almost never go to the Starlight," one person told me. "Once the roof went on, it became the 'Starless Theatre' to me."

"When they put the roof up, I was really upset," said another. "I didn't go in for a long time after that. But things are going to change, you know? And there's nothing you can do to stop it."

Today, the Starlight Theatre is the best known and most consistent venue for gigging opportunities in Terlingua. Thanks to this status, as well as to the venue's history, the significance of the Starlight's transformation extends far beyond the building itself. As South Brewster County continues to grow, and as more and more commercial enterprises have replaced campfires and empty ruins as the seats of the town's social and musical life, the Starlight Theatre has come to symbolize the transformation of Terlingua as a whole. The Starlight did not start this process, of course. It was not the earliest commercial venue in Terlingua, and formal gigs were already taking place when it opened its doors for business. But the symbolic power of the Starlight's transformation—from a storied local hangout into a restaurant frequented by tourists; from a space for spontaneous and inclusive jams into a venue for formal performances; from a ruin with an incomparable view of the night sky into a renovated and bustling business—made the transformation a kind of signpost moment in Terlingua's history, one that is constantly referenced as a major turning point for the town. For some, "the day the roof went on" has come to represent, in a single symbolic moment, the social and musical progression of the reborn town's entire five-decade history: from campfires to bar stools, from starlight to stage lights.

THE ETHNOMUSICOLOGIST John Blacking once wrote that "[c]hanges in the cognitive and social organization of music-making, and in the ways people make sense of music, may signal far-reaching changes in society that could surpass the significance of the musical changes."[9] I often thought about this quote during my time in Terlingua, especially when speaking to longtime residents of the town. For some local musicians, the transition from campfires to commercial spaces represents a major shift, not just in a musical sense, but also in the character of the town itself. They argue that Terlingua music has always been first and foremost about community, about the spirit of participation and noncommercial performance. For them, the gradual shift from jams to gigs is not just a matter of changing venues—it is a threat to Terlingua's identity and to its distinctive community spirit.

"I think the driving force has changed," said Mark Lewis, a fiddle player and river guide who has lived in Terlingua since the early 1990s. "The allure of the stage and the microphone has imprisoned everyone. A lot of people just don't play music on the Porch like they used to." Mark was one of the most active Porch musicians during my time in Terlingua, but he has not played in the commercial venues very often by comparison. "I have no desire to go out and promote myself in the venues down here," he told me. "I get to sit in with people once in a while, and, of course, I love the money. But being onstage, it's isolating. It separates you, when you're up there onstage with a microphone and then there's an audience, instead of a bunch of people around a campfire. It's a totally different world, a totally different paradigm for music. I'm a throwback, I'm a musical Luddite in some ways. 'Cause the recipe that I'm lookin' for, I don't get it on the stage. I get it on the Porch."

I must admit that I had difficulty appreciating Mark's perspective at first. As someone who came to Terlingua from a world where most live music is overtly commercial, I had never lived somewhere with a place like the Porch, a place where I could show up unannounced any day of the week and have a good chance of finding other musicians to play with. To me, Terlingua felt like a jammer's paradise, not a place where the spirit of jamming was under threat. However, as my familiarity with the Terlingua music scene grew, I began to notice that a lot of local musicians rarely play on the Porch, including people who perform regularly in the Starlight and other commercial venues. *Perhaps Mark is right,* I thought to myself.

I asked many of these musicians why they don't participate in Porch music more often. For some, Porch-style jams feel daunting because they require a different set of skills than pre-rehearsed gigs—playing by ear and ad-libbing on

the fly, for instance. Jams also necessitate a different repertoire than onstage performances. The best jammers are able
to quickly gauge the ability levels of the musicians around
them, selecting songs that everyone can learn quickly on the
spot, even when this means playing a lot of simple three-
chord songs so that everyone is included. Sadly, a lot of highly
skilled musicians—both in Terlingua and elsewhere—are
simply unwilling to make this concession. Besides, for those
who make their living from music, adding several hours of
jamming to an already busy schedule of practice and performance can simply be too much for the voice and the fingers
to handle. A few local musicians also pointed out that, while
they place great value on Porch jams, catching a completely
spontaneous musical event is difficult when you live more
than a fifty-mile round-trip from the Porch.

Some long-term Terlingua residents say that Porch jams
are simply not as fun as they were when the town was
smaller. "Back then it wasn't near the kind of zoo it's become," said Laird Considine, who has lived in Terlingua
since the early 1990s. "Sometimes I drive up to the Porch
and there's eighteen guitar pickers and fiddle players and
this and that. And it's all kind of fun and everything, but to
me the good ol' days was when you would go up there and
maybe pull out a mandolin and just play with two or three
people, and there's no tourists standing around with their
iPhones filming it all. It was just a whole different feel to it
back then. Now it's almost like a production or something.
It's noisy and there's too many crazy people and dogs everywhere, and it's just become a scene that, to me, is beyond
what is normally fun to participate in. I'd rather it be more
intimate than *let's all sing some old John Prine song that
everyone knows the words to*, with everyone hollerin' in on
the choruses. That can be fun if you've got enough beers in
you and no one really cares about how it sounds. And sure,
that's a communal thing that's part of our culture going way
back, to all get together and have a hootenanny. I appreciate

that. But those particular moments tend to be moments where I find I'm just flogging away on my instrument breaking strings, just tryin' to be heard in the morass of it all."

Some Terlingua musicians disagree with Mark Lewis that jams deserve to be prioritized over gigs. According to Far Flung founder Mike Davidson, the frustration that sometimes characterizes Porch and campfire jams was one of the factors that led him to form the Terlingua All-Stars. "The campfire stuff was fun," he said, echoing Laird, "but it ended up being chaotic, and some musicians can be a little more perfectionist than others. When you have people getting drunk, and you're trying to play some tunes on acoustic guitar and people start beating on their drums and their plastic tubs and it's all over the place . . . I just can't. The answer to that is electricity and volume."

IT MIGHT APPEAR at this juncture that the Starlight Theatre, in its current manifestation as the primary commercial venue in town, represents the antithesis of the old-school campfire spirit in Terlingua, that in its transformation it has lost everything that once made it a meaningful social space. But reality is not so black-and-white. The Starlight is a commercial space, it's true, but it also functions as a community center in ways that are not so clearly motivated by commercial interests. It regularly provides space for local charity benefits, for example, as well as for poetry readings, art exhibits, and a range of other local-oriented events. The community garden gets its supply of rainwater free of charge from the Starlight's roof via cisterns that sit along the west side of the building. The Starlight's current owner, Bill Ivey, allows a number of people to live in his Ghost Town properties rent-free under the stipulation that tenants help to maintain the integrity of the historic buildings in which they reside. It is far too simplistic, in other words, to neatly conflate commercialism with social degradation and anti-commercialism with community.

The same can be said for the music that is made in the Starlight Theatre today. While Porch jams might be particularly well suited for cultivating the bonds of community, a gig can foster the same feelings when musicians and audiences value those feelings. Buckner Cooke, who booked music at the Starlight from 2013 to 2016, once told me the story of his "favorite moment of Terlingua music." Butch Hancock, a Far Flung boatman and one of the only Terlingua musicians to ever garner considerable renown outside Terlingua, had just concluded a gig at the Starlight Theatre with another musician from out of town.

"They played their set," Buckner recalled, "and Jim Vance [pseudonym] started to put his stuff away. Well, Darren [a longtime Terlingua river guide] was standing over at the bar, and he kind of stumbled forward a bit and said, 'You didn't play "Boxcars."' And Jim Vance said, 'We don't take requests.' And Darren said, 'I'm not talking to you, I'm talking to *you*.' And he pointed at Butch, who he had known for decades. He said, 'You and I got a history, and you didn't play "Boxcars."' Butch had already unplugged his guitar, but he said, 'You know what, Darren, you're right.' So he sat down at the closest table, and off microphone, with his guitar unplugged, he started to play 'Boxcars,' and we all just moved in and sat around him. He probably played eight more songs that night while we all just sat around him listening. That doesn't happen when Butch plays in Austin or anywhere else. That only happens *here*. There were only a dozen or so people in the Starlight, and it was one of the greatest things I've ever seen in my life. To me, that's a defining difference in the Terlingua scene. The intimacy, the lack of ego that goes into something like that, is *far* different than any other music scene I've ever been a part of."

Buckner's story demonstrates that it is the attitude, rather than the setting or the style of play, that ultimately gives a musical performance its power. Life in Terlingua may never again be centered around campfires, but Terlingua residents continue to demonstrate how that same spirit—that solidarity and camaraderie that gave the early fires so much meaning—can still be cultivated, no matter where or in what way the music is made.

As for the original Starlight mural, the one sketched in chalk? It turns out it is still there. Rob and Angie Dean, the founding owners of the Starlight Theatre Restaurant & Bar, must have been well aware of the symbolic power permeating the dilapidated building that was their charge. Rather than destroying the mural during the renovation process, they instead chose to build a separate wall on top of it, thereby ensuring that the memorial of young Terlingua would be forever preserved. There it remains, like the campfires, lying just beneath the surface.

CHAPTER 2

IN THE INCUBATOR

"WHEN I FIRST CAME HERE, I did not play in public," Carol Whitney confessed during a break between songs. "I would barely play music in front of anybody. But then I stepped onto the Porch and Moses was like, 'Get that guitar out! Sing a song! Show us what you've got!' So I have to credit this place and these people. There's no way in hell I'd be out there playing the Starlight for a whole night show if it wasn't for Moses."

It was a Tuesday afternoon in late March, and I had dropped by Carol's trailer in the hopes we might trade a few songs before she departed for New Mexico for the summer. Like many Terlinguans, Carol lives in the Big Bend on a seasonal basis, spending the cooler months in Terlingua but retreating north each spring to avoid the oppressive summer heat. We sat together in the shade of a young cottonwood tree, guitars in our laps, and took turns playing songs while savoring the last few days of pleasant temperatures before the mercury began its inevitable climb into the triple digits.

Carol is small in stature but boisterous in character. A motorcycle injury has left her with chronic back pain and a slight hunch in her posture, but these ailments seem to vanish whenever she picks up a guitar. Carol's eyes sparkle with enthusiasm behind her glasses whenever she talks about music. She had been a "closet player" for years before she came to the Big Bend—in other words, she never performed in front of other people. She credits the Terlingua community for coaxing her out of her shell, for providing her with the opportunities and encouragement she needed to begin playing in public.

I asked Carol if she remembered the first time she played with other musicians, and she responded without hesitation. "Oh, definitely! It was on the Porch. I'd been here for probably six weeks, and I'd been watching and listening to all these people, and I thought, *you know, I'm just gonna take my guitar up there and see what happens.* I was super nervous. And the first thing that happened is Moses gave me shit! He said, 'You've been here for six weeks and this is the first time you've brought out your guitar? Play something, girl! What'cha got?' So we played a bunch of songs together, and it was just such a *rush* . . . it's like speaking a different language with a bunch of new people who speak this language that you thought only you knew. It was a beautiful thing. It was fun! Experiences like that really got me over the hump of being afraid to play with other musicians and in front of other people."

"And now you're playing gigs!" I said. Carol smiled. In a few hours, she would be onstage at the Starlight where she was booked as the featured musician for the evening.

"You know," she recalled, "when I was a kid, I always imagined what it would be like to actually get up on a stage and perform for people, just how cool that would be. It's something I never thought would happen. And now, for me to go to the Starlight, to set up my shit, to play my music all night, have people *tip* me for it and come up and tell me they thought it was great? For me, that's a ten-year-old girl's dream come true. And it definitely took a lot of work to get there, but I never thought in a million years . . ." Carol paused for a moment as she reflected on how far she had come. "You know, if you'd asked me ten years ago if

I thought this would ever happen, I would have laughed at ya."

Not long ago, Carol had no idea that Terlingua even existed. Her first trip to the Big Bend was in 2011, when, like most people, she came to visit the national park. She stopped over at the Starlight for a bite to eat, completely unaware that the town she had wandered into was a veritable hotbed of musical activity. She certainly had no inkling of the transformative role that Terlingua would soon play in her own life. Carol's first experience on the Porch was very much like my own: quiet at first, but before long, the music took over. Like me, Carol was blown away by the amount of music she witnessed. She wanted to know why it was happening, but even more, she wanted to know how she could be a part of it. That first evening on the Porch proved to be a major catalyst for Carol. She now spends several months in Terlingua every winter, and her annual visit has become something of a musical pilgrimage.

"If you had never come to Terlingua," I asked her, "do you think you would've found a way to do it? To start gigging?"

"I honestly don't know," Carol admitted, absentmindedly strumming her guitar while she spoke. "I do know this was definitely a huge catalyst for it. The first gig I ever played was a Starlight brunch the second year I came down. Alex is the one I credit for that. It was nine o'clock in the morning on a Sunday, and he comes banging on the door." Carol pounded her fist on the picnic table to imitate Alex's frantic knocking. "He says, 'Carol! You up yet? They got nobody playing at the Starlight this morning, you want to play?' And I'm *panicked*!" Carol thumped her hand rapidly on her chest to indicate her racing heartbeat. "And so I'm like, 'Uh, what time do I gotta start?' And Alex says, 'Eleven! Two hours from now!' And it's like . . . *Oh, shit* . . . 'Okay, I'm going!' And I went up there and I *did* it. And it was *great*, you know, it was all locals and it was super quiet and it was perfect.

And Alex knew that, he knew it was the perfect place for me to start." I smiled at the thought of Alex—one of the more experienced performers in Terlingua—banging on Carol's trailer door on a Sunday morning to offer her a gig that he easily could have taken for himself.

"That must have been intentional on his part," I suggested.

"Oh, it was *totally* intentional on his part!" Carol said. "There's a lot of that in this town, musicians helping other musicians. It's like you and me with Dave at the fire the other night. That's how it works."

I nodded. A few nights before, Carol and I had been sitting around a campfire at the RV park with a half-dozen other people when we discovered that Dave had recently begun learning the ukulele. He was hesitant to play in front of the group, but Carol and I eventually convinced him to bring his instrument to the fire. We took turns leading him through some simple three-chord songs, taking each one slowly and calling out the chords while he worked his way through the progressions. It was Dave's first time making music with other people, and it was obvious that the experience had made a big impression on him.

"Do you remember the giggle he had after the first song that we played?" Carol asked. "He was giggling like a kid! He was like, 'That was so *fun*!' That is how it works around here. He shows up and he plays a couple songs, and then next year we'll drag him up to the Porch and he'll play a few more songs. Nobody cares if Dave only knows three chords, or if you have to tell him all the chords to the song. It's cool, you know? I've never seen another place where musicians nurture each other like that." I agreed with Carol. I had been witnessing similar displays of musical camaraderie since my first day in town. It was one of the things that had drawn me to Terlingua in the first place.

"But you know, music *should* be like that," Carol continued, her enthusiasm audibly growing. "Music *should* be

Carol Whitney performs at the Starlight Theatre, 2014.

something that bonds people together, not a competition to say *mine's better than yours*, or *I'm better than you*, and all that shit. And you know, there's been some really bad musicians who have come through here. But they're still welcomed on the Porch, and everybody plays with them, and they get to have their time. And it's okay, people don't judge 'em. That's the thing I love about music in Terlingua. It's very inclusive. It's not all about me showcasing my music and the rest of you listening to it. Instead it's about a collaborative effort and people playing together. It's very inclusive and it's very supportive."

Carol is not alone in her testimony. Many of the musicians who frequent the Porch, the Starlight, and the other venues in town have had formative musical experiences while in Terlingua: gaining the confidence to perform in public, learning to play along with other musicians, playing by ear rather than notation, improvising solos, landing a first paying gig, writing an original song, or even recording a debut album. Even I, an experienced performer with years of formal musical training, was given chances to grow musically that I had never enjoyed in other music scenes. For me, going to Terlingua was like going back to school.

How is this possible? How is Terlingua so good at cultivating musicianship, so good at encouraging musicians like Carol and allowing them to shine? Is it a fluke? Some accident of the town's history? Or is there something more deliberate at work here? When I first visited Terlingua in spring 2013 and took a seat on the Porch, I was astonished by the amount of music I witnessed. Here I was, out in the desert—a hundred miles from nowhere, in what seemed like one of the unlikeliest places imaginable—and people were making music as if it were as normal as breathing. As I would later learn, some of these Porch musicians had made careers in music. A few had spent decades recording and touring the world. Sitting right next to them on those long wooden benches were people who were still learning to strum their first few chords.

It did not take me long to realize that something special was happening in Terlingua. Why is such a high percentage of the Terlingua population musically active? And what is it about the town's character that drives all this activity? As it turns out, I was not the only person to take notice.

"That's why I keep coming back here year after year," Carol said unequivocally as she packed up her gear in preparation for her gig. "Terlingua is an incubator. A very rare music incubator."

IN THE INCUBATOR

"In order to be an incubator," Carol continued, "you have to accept baby musicians, or people who play something different than what you want, or who are still developing their skills or learning to play with other musicians. You have to accept them and welcome them."

If there is one word that is most commonly used by Terlingua musicians to describe their town's music scene, it is "welcoming." This is especially true for those on the less experienced end of the spectrum. I spoke with dozens of residents who recounted formative experiences they had had while starting out as musicians.

"It never would've occurred to me to even own a guitar before I moved here," said June Rapp, a longtime Terlingua resident who started playing music after moving to the Big Bend. "I just always figured I wasn't musical in that way. It never even entered my mind."

Ed Hegarty had a similar experience. A Terlingua resident for more than a decade when I first met him, Ed was a regular on the Porch during my time in town, and he always seemed to listen intently whenever music was taking place. Ed had no musical experience prior to moving to the Big Bend, but the daily spectacle of music making eventually compelled him to give music a try. Not long after I arrived in Terlingua, Ed bought a mountain dulcimer and began teaching himself to play.

"I had no musical inclination before I came here," said Ed. "But it looked like everyone was having such a great time, and I wanted to be a part of what everybody was doing. And since you can't hardly kick over a rock in this desert without uncovering a good guitar player, it just seemed natural to try and join in." I asked Ed if he thought he ever would have picked up an instrument without first moving to Terlingua. "Oh no," he replied emphatically, practically brushing away my question. "There may be other places in this country or in this state that are as open and welcoming as Terlingua, but I haven't lived in any of them yet. This is the only place where people have encouraged me to develop whatever artistic skill I might have hidden away." Ed smiled and patted his dulcimer as it rested in his lap. "Without the music community that is here, I wouldn't be playing this instrument today the way I do."

I have always been impressed by Ed's courage. It takes guts to begin playing in public, no matter the context in which one's musical journey begins. But to jump into the fire as Ed has—to be a complete beginner and show up to a place like the Porch, where the level of musicianship is often quite high—would have terrified me as a young musician. Ed, however, insists that it feels different in Terlingua.

"The folks who can really rip, they don't care if there's a guy on the periphery trying to keep up," he said. "No, I have always felt very encouraged here. Most of the folks who make up the fabric of our music scene are welcoming to every beginner, whether they're playing an instrument or singing off-key or even just banging a bottle cap on a bottle. You don't have to prove yourself to be competent or even confident to join in. And that attitude fosters growth."

The Porch is the most popular site for jams in Terlingua today, and as such it has become one of the primary places where beginning musicians are encouraged to perform. For Carol Whitney, the Porch was the place where she began her journey from closet player to public performer. "The Porch gave me the opportunity to play with other musicians," she said. "Before, I'd always just played by myself. But now, to sit down and make music with a group of people? Oh my god, that's as good as it gets! And it's an everyday thing here. You can take your guitar up on the Porch any day of the week and you'll find somebody to play music with. That's unheard of. When I leave Terlingua in the spring, I know that's not gonna happen again until I come back."

While many Terlingua musicians have had their earliest musical experiences on the Porch, not everyone finds its often raucous musical atmosphere appealing. Fortunately, there are a number of other options in town for beginners who want to try their hand at making music in a casual setting. In recent years, a number of song circles have sprung up around Terlingua. Unlike the Porch, where there frequently are onlookers and where the overall volume can get quite loud, song circles provide a quieter, more intimate environment where musicians can take turns performing solo or in small groups for their fellow participants. Local artist, songwriter, and off-grid pioneer Collie Ryan has been responsible for organizing a number of these song circles, and she too emphasizes the importance of opening the circle to everyone, regardless of musical ability.

"What I like with the Sunday circles," Collie said, "and what is important to the spirit of the music, is that it's open to everybody. If you're not cool, and you don't do good, you still got a place. You might get better, you might not. You might bore us to death for four years. But you still got a space, 'cause that's the spirit of it."

Terlingua residents Mary Diesel and June Rapp host another song circle twice a month in a quiet side room of La Kiva. Like Collie, they too wanted to create a space for music that was highly inclusive. "To me the Porch is a lot about the instruments," said June. "But in the song circle, you don't have to be a musician. It's more about singing than it is about instruments, and a cappella is encouraged. A lot of people really like to sing, but they would *never* sing in a million years on the Porch. We wanted everyone to be able to participate."

Regular events like song circles and Porch jams, both of which allow inexperienced musicians to participate without the pressure of satisfying an audience, play a key role in making Terlingua so highly musical. However, Terlingua's encouragement of beginners does not end with these events, and this is another reason why the music scene is so rare. In most scenes, inexperienced musicians who are fortunate enough to have access to beginner-friendly spaces like song circles and jams also tend to be confined to those spaces, expected to hone their musical chops in certain designated settings before proceeding to other, more "advanced" performance contexts like gigs or the recording studio. Hence the idea of the "closet" player: first you put in enough time until you reach a certain level of skill, and only then are you allowed to move onto the stage. Sadly, many aspiring performers who follow this model never make it past the closet.

This is not the case in Terlingua. Rather than being confined to "safe" spaces like Porch jams and song circles, beginners in Terlingua are regularly given opportunities that in most music scenes are reserved exclusively for more advanced performers. "This place is like that," Carol observed. "It'll let the campfire player go to the next level. That's the kind of thing that happens here that never happens anywhere else." Among these opportunities is the chance to play onstage. In Terlingua, musicians who are just beginning their musical journeys are regularly invited onto the stage to perform in front of audiences. Local fiddler Anna Oakley recounted her first experience playing in public, which occurred not long after she moved to Terlingua and only a few years after picking up a fiddle for the first time.

"It was at the Boathouse," Anna said. "Jim and Pablo were playing, and it was really casual, just a few microphones set up out in the back. But I was still totally nervous like it's Carnegie Hall or something." Anna had learned a handful of Irish tunes, but she had only ever played along with recordings. "I'd never actually played with another person before and I wasn't really sure what to do," Anna said. "So I just hammered through those songs like I do in my room by myself. I don't know, I just figured that was what I was supposed to do! But then Pablo started belting out the lyrics and I stopped playing, and then he stopped singing and took a lead [solo]. But when they looked back at me I didn't know how to start playing again, 'cause I had never given anybody a lead before! Jim was telling me, 'You gotta listen! You gotta stop, give somebody a lead and then listen for when to come

back in.' That was really good training for me to start playing with other people."

In Terlingua, less experienced musicians are also encouraged to go into the recording studio, an opportunity that in
most music scenes is even less open to amateurs than the
stage. Remarkably, Terlingua has had a full-service recording
studio since 1995—longer than it has had a school, a well-
stocked grocery store, a bank, or even a public water utility.
Ted Arbogast, the founder, owner, and recording engineer at
Studio Butte (a play on "Study Butte," one of the old mining
camps that has been incorporated into present-day Terlingua), has recorded more than fifty complete albums at his
studio on Terlingua Ranch in the quarter century that it has
been in operation. Many of the town's resident musicians
have recorded there, a roster encompassing all skill levels
from rank beginners to professionals.

Ted does not run Studio Butte for a living, but it is a far
cry from a hobbyist's makeshift garage studio. On the outside, it is modest, a simple four-walled adobe that resembles
many of the other structures in the area. Upon entering,
however, one is greeted by soundproof rooms, full spreads
of equipment for both digital and analog recording, and a
soundboard that would make some professional recording
engineers green with envy. Ted also runs his studio differently from a lot of engineers I have worked with. Many engineers prefer to remain in the background, taking care of all
the technical details but expecting their clients to make the
majority of the creative decisions (instrumentation and so
on) that are an inherent part of the recording process. Ted,
on the other hand, is much more hands-on.

"I've always been someone who arranges in bands," Ted
told me. "I just love that type of creation. That's what inspires me to run this studio. People come through the door,
and when they leave, they're always like, 'Whoa! I didn't
know it could sound like this! I didn't know it could be like

that!' I've never been able to write a song, so the next best thing is to be a kind of midwife for other people's songs, to help bring them out and let them live."

Ted's creative approach makes him the perfect person to run a beginner-friendly studio in a place like Terlingua. While his style might not be the right fit for everyone, for musicians unfamiliar with the recording process, his input often proves invaluable. Such is the case for June Rapp, a longtime Terlingua resident who has recorded four albums of original songs at Studio Butte (and who previously admitted to "never having considered owning a guitar" before moving to the Big Bend). I met June not long after I arrived in Terlingua, when Ted called me into the studio to record some saxophone tracks for her third album. As a newcomer in town, I had been busy meeting musicians and making the rounds at all the local music venues, so I was surprised that I hadn't run into June before. When I mentioned this to June, she gave me a sheepish look.

"I don't have a lot of confidence performing live," she admitted. June then explained that for her, that was precisely what she enjoyed about recording—it gave her an alternative way to get her songs out into the world. "It has been *wonderful*," she said. "This has made it possible for me to share my music. And I'm *so* grateful to Ted for that. Ted charged like twelve bucks an hour for my first album, so it wasn't financially out of the question to make a CD. And my songs, they have always been quite basic and simple, but he fleshed them out, added instruments, and made a much bigger sound than I could've ever imagined. It was a kick! It's such a surprise to find yourself in a recording studio hearing yourself through the headphones for the first time. In some ways, it was a struggle for me 'cause I was nervous. But for the most part, it was just a wonderful, *wonderful* experience."

Ultimately, like so many other aspects of my time in Terlingua, what I saw at Studio Butte forced me to fundamentally rethink my long-held assumptions about what

Studio Butte recording studio on Terlingua Ranch, 2016.

Ted Arbogast on the boards at Studio Butte, 2016.

recording studios are all about. I had always taken for granted that musicians develop their skills along a strictly linear trajectory. First you learn the basics, then you practice those basics until a level of competency is reached. At this point, you begin performing in public, perhaps at open-mic nights or some other beginner-friendly venue, and you continue on this path until you are good enough to finally start landing your own paying gigs. Only once you have proven yourself as a competent performing musician would you ever consider going into the recording studio. This was the path that all the musicians I knew had followed, and, as far as I was concerned, this was how it was *supposed* to be done. It had never occurred to me that a recording studio could be so much more than that. In its more than twenty-five years of operation, Studio Butte has never made very much money. But making money has never been Ted's goal. In the true Terlingua spirit, he was after something far greater—to provide an entry point into the absolute joy that is musical expression. Here I was in an endless sea of desert, looking on as Studio Butte operated on a radically different principle than any I had ever seen.

PLAYING TOGETHER

It should be clear by now that Terlingua excels at providing less experienced musicians with ample opportunities to perform. However, Terlingua's ultimate status as a music incubator relies on more than simply getting those musicians playing. A crucial part of the town's success is that these beginners get to play right alongside the pros.

In a 2013 TED Talk, bass guitarist and music educator Victor Wooten spoke about the importance of allowing beginners to play with experts, arguing that we should teach music to children the same way we teach them to speak. "If you think about how you learned [your first language]," Wooten said, "you realize you weren't taught it. People just spoke to you. But the coolest thing—and this is where it gets interesting—is you were allowed to speak back. Now, if I take the music example, in most cases our beginners are not allowed to play with the better people. You're stuck in a beginning class, you have to remain there a few years until you elevate into the intermediate and then advanced, and after you graduate the advanced class, you still have to go out and pay a lot of dues. But with language, to use a musical term, even as a baby, you're 'jamming' with professionals all the time . . . . No one says 'I can't talk to you, you gotta go over there, when you're older then I can speak to you.' That doesn't happen."

In Wooten's view, one of the primary reasons that most people progress faster when learning to speak than when learning music is that we learn to speak by communicating with experts rather than fellow beginners. This "jamming with professionals" is an uncommon approach to musical training in the Western world, but in Terlingua, it happens on a daily basis. Here, advanced and inexperienced musicians are not separated into different musical spaces, but rather perform alongside each other all the time.

I asked Bruce Salmon, who was one of Terlingua's more experienced performers during the time I lived there and who has spent most of his life touring and performing professionally, if he knew of any other music scenes where musicians of widely varying ability levels play together so regularly. "Not really," Bruce admitted. "It's a bit like being at a folk festival, at a jam in the parking lot or the campground. It reminds me of that. But even at some of those, it's like people are trying to stake their turf more. I feel like here, everybody is really in service to the shared fandango, even the people pitchin' in who are pros."

Buckner Cooke agreed. Buckner was responsible for booking music at the Starlight Theatre while I was in Terlingua. An ex-Austinite, he was immediately struck when he moved to the Big Bend by how different it was from the better-known music scenes of the Texas Hill Country. "There's too much of a sense of ego within the Hill Country scenes," he opined. "I think a lot of that ego gets lost when you come down here. The hierarchy here is far looser than what you see in Austin or Kerrville. There are musicians there who will *never* end up playing with other members of the scene. But in Terlingua, that's a *part* of the scene. I mean, you can go up onstage on New Year's Day and throw in with Butch Hancock! That kind of thing just doesn't happen anywhere else. There's a certain intimacy in that, and it's something that we all share, even as members of the audience. Here in Terlingua, the simple fact that music is *happening* means you can be a part of it."

In order for this approach to be successful, the advanced musicians in town must obviously be on board. I've experienced some music scenes where it was typical for the better musicians to avoid the kinds of places where less experienced musicians were known to congregate. Take open mics, for example. Open-mic nights are a common event throughout the country, and virtually everywhere they take place they provide opportunities for less experienced musicians to perform. They are often treated as training grounds, places where inexperienced musicians can practice performing onstage with the goal of eventually transitioning to paying gigs and other professional performances. Advanced musicians rarely play at open mics, and when they do, they tend to treat them as practice sessions for other performances, just as an experienced comedian might try out new material in a small room. In any case, open mics are usually considered to be a transitional phase in a musician's journey, something you graduate from rather than aspire to.

On the surface, open mics in Terlingua are the same as everywhere else. A sign-up sheet is located next to the stage, and performance slots last anywhere from ten minutes to a half-hour. That, however, is where the similarities end.

For one thing, Terlingua open mics are profoundly casual from an organizational standpoint, with the sign-up sheet providing a structure that is, at best, only loosely followed. Rather than taking turns, musicians usually end up sitting in on one another's sets, and at times this becomes such a perpetual part of the music that events begin to look less and less like conventional open mics and more like Porch jams with sign-up sheets.

The biggest difference in Terlingua open mics, however, is the caliber of musicians who perform at them. The best musicians in town play open mics, treating them as if they were every bit as important as their own paying gigs. This was something that Jim Keaveny realized immediately upon moving to Terlingua. "Musicians in this town are not so much career-driven," he said. "I used to tell people, 'Oh, I don't do open mics anymore,' after I'd started touring and doing my own thing. But in this town I *will* play them because open mics in Terlingua are more about people just getting together and having a party and sharing songs."

Entertainment booker Buckner Cooke noticed it, too. "The level of musicianship at the open mics here is far greater than what you'll see in most other places," he said. "Take Austin, for example. Ian Moore, Bob Schneider—you know, the leading lights in the Austin scene—they're not gonna wander into an open mic in Austin. But here? You're gonna have Pat O'Bryan and Trevor Hickle and Butch Hancock show up, and it's like, *Oh my god! This could go on for another two hours and nobody would mind! But this . . . this is an open mic!* That's the kind of thing that just doesn't happen anywhere else."

It might seem at this juncture that Terlingua's music scene is geared exclusively toward amateur musicians and that those who already possess a decent amount of musical experience are unlikely to find many opportunities there. However, while this rare musical climate does provide

Open mic at the Boathouse Bar, Terlingua, Texas, 2016.

beginners with unprecedented access to a wide variety of performance contexts, this same climate also affords advanced musicians their own fair share of opportunities for growth.

This is something I experienced firsthand. I arrived in the Big Bend with one music degree in hand and another in the works, along with a good deal of performing experience in jazz and the classical tradition. In Terlingua, I got to play a much wider variety of styles, including country, blues, folk, old-time, bluegrass, norteño, and cumbia. Significantly, a number of these styles do not normally feature saxophone, so I likely would not have enjoyed the same opportunities to perform them in a larger music scene where conventional instrumentation would be easier to come by. (After all, no country artist in Nashville would hire a saxophonist when they have a hundred fiddlers and pedal steel players on speed dial.) In Terlingua, I got to play in duos for the first time, learning how to assume the role of backup musician to a singer-songwriter—another opportunity not extended to many saxophonists. Thanks to the gentle prodding and encouragement of one local performer, I took my first clarinet solos in public, and I managed to stumble my way through the odd tune on fiddle, mandolin, and washtub bass. A closet guitar player before arriving in Terlingua, I got to sing and play the guitar with other musicians, another first. I learned the ins and outs of Porch music: how to play effective rhythm guitar, how to back up soloists between verses, how to end songs and signal changes in the form. I even made my first meager attempts at improvised guitar solos. Eventually, I played my first-ever guitar gig at the Boathouse Bar, which was also my first-ever solo gig on any instrument. Put simply, although I had been an active musician since childhood, during my two years in Terlingua I was treated to a far wider variety of musical experiences than I had enjoyed at any other time in my life.

Many of Terlingua's more advanced musicians shared my experience. Chris Baker came to the Big Bend with extensive formal training in classical flute performance, having studied with some of the premiere flutists in the country. It wasn't until she moved to Terlingua in the early 1990s, however, that she learned how to play by ear and improvise—skills that she now uses in the vast majority of her performances. "I played with a rock band for a while before moving to Terlingua," Chris recalled, "and when I had to take a solo, it was like torture for me because I wasn't very good. Then once I got here, I just started playing everything by ear. So the gift that playing in Terlingua has given me is a good ear. Now, I feel I have the confidence to basically sit in with anybody."

A full-time musician, Bruce Salmon has spent his entire adult life onstage with a band. He credits Terlingua, however, with providing him with the opportunities he needed to become a solo performer—an important skill, from a financial perspective, for anyone who makes a living playing music.

Bruce went even further, saying that Terlingua helped him gain a different perspective on what it means to be a professional musician. "The thing I really like about Terlingua," he said, "is that there's not elitist snobbery by people who are going for it professionally relative to people who are playing at some other level. It's way more inclusive and celebratory. And weirdly enough, that has given me a better basis for being a professional. Staying humble, and realizing that you're not all that—to me, that is part of communicating music in an effective way. I think being here keeps people humble in a way that's really healthy. It doesn't keep you humble by humiliation. Instead, it's more about just realizing that there are a lot of people in the world, and everybody has something to offer and you're just one of them."

THE WESTERN OBSESSION WITH "TALENT"

The musicians who live and perform in Terlingua arrived in the desert with a wide range of experience levels. Some, like Carol, were longtime closet musicians intimidated by the thought of playing in public. Others had never picked up a musical instrument before moving to South County. At the other end of the spectrum, a number of Terlingua musicians had years of experience writing, recording, and touring as professional musicians before moving to the Big Bend. Of all the people I spoke with—beginners and experts, newcomers and longtime residents, performers and enthusiastic listeners—I did not encounter a single person who disagreed with Carol's basic assertion that Terlingua is an incubator of musicians. Even those who had previously lived and performed in places that might subjectively be considered "better" music scenes believe that Terlingua is uncommonly successful in cultivating musical participation across a wide range of skill levels.

Why is Terlingua so unique in this respect? Why is the encouragement of amateur musicians not a more common part of American musical life? As it turns out, the notion expressed by Bruce Salmon above—that "everybody has something to offer" when it comes to music—is not a very common sentiment in the United States. On the contrary, it is often assumed that some percentage of the population, and perhaps even a majority of the population, is inherently unmusical. I've lost count of the number of times I've heard someone say something along the lines of "I wish I could sing, but I am completely tone deaf" or "I love music, but I don't have a musical bone in my body," expressions that, in effect, dismiss even the remotest possibility of musical participation. I expect that most readers will have heard these expressions as well. Perhaps they have even uttered something similar about themselves. If so, they would not be alone. In much of the developed world, it is assumed that music in the public sphere should be left to specialists, those select few "talented" individuals who are believed to possess some rarified natural aptitude for music. Everyone else is confined to the sidelines, deemed "untalented" and there-fore unworthy or incapable of joining in.

This is by no means a universal phenomenon. As Henry Kingsbury observed in his book *Music, Talent, and Performance*, "The notion of 'talent' is so fundamental to Western thinking about human musicality that it perhaps still needs to be emphasized that differentials in musical or esthetic talent are not to be found everywhere."[1] Indeed, researchers in the social sciences have long known that our culturally inscribed thoughts about talent are far from universal. As early as 1958, American anthropologist John Messenger, working among the Anang Ibibio people of Nigeria, reported that the idea of a person being inherently unmusical did not exist among the Anang Ibibio. "We search in vain for the 'non-musical' person," he wrote, "finding it difficult to make inquiries about tone deafness and its assumed ef-fects because the Anang language possesses no comparable concept. . . . They will not admit, as we tried so hard to get them to, that there are those who lack the requisite abilities."[2] A few decades later, anthropologist Steven Feld found that the same was true for the Kaluli of Papua New Guinea, who treat musicality the same way they treat other forms of communication such as language and gesture—as an innate part of being human. "We in the West assume some sort of necessity for symbolic competence in the verbal and gestural modes," Feld wrote, "[but] we assume no such thing for other varieties of symbolic competence [such as music], and therefore utilize culturally invested notions (like 'talent') to explain or rationalize stratifications in awareness, expressive production, and interpretation. Nothing parallel exists among the Kaluli."[3] The British ethnomusicologist John Blacking also observed this during his research among the Venda people of South Africa. According to Blacking, the idea that some people are innately musical and others are not is "diametrically opposed to the Venda idea that all normal human beings are capable of musical performance."[4] In his book *How Musical is Man?*, he compared his experience among the Venda to his own upbringing in the European tradition. "It may well be," he reflected, "that the social and cultural inhibitions that prevent the flowering of musical genius are more significant than any individual ability that may seem to promote it."[5]

Research in the cognitive sciences also suggests that much of what we regard as talent is actually the result of regular exposure and practice. Psychologist John A. Sloboda criticized what he referred to as the dominant "folk psychology" of the Western world that suggests that musical ability is largely innate, arguing instead that "the capacity for musical accomplishment of one sort or another [is] a species-defining characteristic."[6] Psychologist Earl Hunt agreed, suggesting that the development of ability, including musical ability, is principally due to environmental factors. "Because the acquisition of expertise requires substantial effort," he wrote in *The Cambridge Handbook of Expertise and Expert Performance,* "the social support provided during the learning phase is extremely important. . . . Because expertise requires motivation and support, society has considerable leverage in deciding what types of expertise will be developed."[7]

In citing the above authors, I do not mean to suggest that innate musical ability is a complete myth. To the contrary, I have met a number of people in my life, as I expect we all have, who seem to show some inborn predisposition toward music. Rather, my point is that the significance of natural talent to a person's overall musical potential and development is profoundly overstated in Western society at large. The unfortunate result is that only a small percentage of the population believes they are capable of performing music in any meaningful way. Rather than allowing everyone the opportunity to experience the joy of creating music—as do many other culture groups around the world—we instead restrict musical participation to a special class we have deemed worthy—the "talented."

Why do we treat music this way? Why in Western societies is public music making considered the domain of the singularly skilled? After all, we take a very different approach to other forms of socializing and communication. (Imagine, for example, if only professional public speakers were given social license to converse!) It should be noted that this has not always been the case. In fact, music's shift from a widely shared social activity to the exclusive domain of professionals occurred relatively late in European and American history. As recently as the late nineteenth century, most music making in Western Europe and the United States was done by amateurs.[8] Many of the canonical composers whose names are familiar—Mozart, Vivaldi, Chopin—spent the majority of their time writing music intended for amateur performers. The famous symphonies of Beethoven were premiered by orchestras filled with amateur musicians. Until the early twentieth century, performing parlor music at home alongside one's friends and family was one of the most popular forms of entertainment in the United States and Europe. Musical performance was not an activity reserved for a specialist class—it was an activity for everyone.

The development of new audio technologies in the late 1800s and early 1900s began to profoundly change how people in the developed world thought about music. In 1877, American inventor Thomas Edison introduced the world to his phonograph, the first machine capable of reproducing and playing back recorded audio. Edison's machine was revolutionary, but it had one major limitation: the wax and tinfoil cylinders onto which it recorded could not be copied. This problem was solved ten years later with the release of Emile Berliner's gramophone. Berliner's device was similar to Edison's phonograph, but it recorded onto a brand new type of disc—a predecessor to the modern vinyl record—that was easier to ship and store and could be quickly and efficiently mass-produced from a single master recording.[9]

It would be difficult to overstate just how dramatically this new audio technology transformed music in the Western world. The gramophone, and later the radio (the commercial development of which began in the early 1920s), had a somewhat paradoxical double effect, encouraging people to become more musical in some ways and less musical in others. On one hand, the wide dissemination of such technologies—across all geographies and, eventually, all income levels—made music more accessible to a greater number of people. It was suddenly possible for a farmer in rural Kansas to hear a performance of a Brahms symphony, a North Carolina fiddler, or a Delta blues singer, all in the comfort of his own home. According to Mark Katz in his book *Capturing Sound*, some observers at the time even believed that by increasing the average listener's exposure to music, these new technologies would "help America become a truly musical nation."[10]

However, by separating music from the previously essential act of performing it, these same technologies also contributed to a major shift in *how* listeners engaged with music, even as the frequency and variety of their listening increased. Rather than being an activity in which to participate, music became a product that could be passively bought and consumed. In *Selling Sounds*, David Suisman argued that Berliner's gramophone created a new "social division" between those who performed music and those who listened to it. "Consumers," he wrote, "assimilated the idea of music as issuing from an automatic machine (such as a phonograph or player-piano), detached from human labor, and fixed in objects (such as records or piano rolls), portable and storable, and independent of time and place. Music, which had once been produced in the home, by hand, was now something to be purchased, like a newspaper or ready-to-wear dress."[11]

The practical effect of this shift is that many listeners began using recorded music as a replacement for their own live performances, rather than as a supplement to them. The influential American band composer and director John Philip Sousa expressed concern that this would happen, arguing during testimony at a 1906 congressional hearing that new technologies for recording and producing music were "discouraging many Americans from doing their own singing and playing."[12] In hindsight, his fears seem well founded. "The manufacturers of player-pianos and phonographs," wrote Suisman, "ushered in a new cultural order in which people became closer to music in some respects and more distanced from it in others. With player-piano rolls and phonograph records, it was possible to hear expert renditions of Beethoven or Verdi in the intimacy of one's own home, at any time. . . . Despite hopes that the enhanced availability of music would fuel musical training, in reality it often meant simply that the actual human labor of making music was now accomplished somewhere else, by specialists."[13]

With access to expert performances increasingly at listeners' fingertips, amateur music making began to wane in popularity in the United States around the turn of the twentieth century. Contemporary observers reported a decline in social music making from the 1890s to the 1920s, while music teachers reported losing students as more and more households acquired phonographs.[14] Meanwhile, as radio and record sales skyrocketed, the American piano business went into massive decline. In 1909, there were three hundred piano manufacturers in the United States; by the late 1920s, that number had dropped to eighty-one.[15]

Today, the Western world still lives with the legacy of this technological turn in music history. Even while the act of listening has become more democratized than ever before—a wider variety of music is now available to a broader number of people than at any point in human history—the act of *performing* music has moved in the opposite direction, becoming instead a meritocracy, a domain for specialists in which only the most talented or most skilled are considered good enough to make music in the public forum. The music we hear live and on the radio is perhaps more "perfect" as a result. But as Sousa foresaw more than a century ago, something significant was lost in the exchange. "The price we pay for that perfection," musicologist Christopher Small observed in his book *Musicking*, "is that the majority of people are considered not to have the ability to take an active part in a musical performance. They are excluded from the magic world of the musicians."[16]

Terlingua might be an uncommonly musical place by American standards, but it is not immune to the country's broader societal conceptions about talent. During my time in the Big Bend, I heard people express many of the same sentiments that I have heard elsewhere—"I have no musical ability," and so forth. I also spoke with a number of self-taught musicians who, when they found out about my own musical background, felt the need to apologize for not being "real" musicians, or who were quick to confess that they lacked formal training or knowledge of music theory, as if these gaps in their experience somehow undermined their legitimacy as performers. Many of the beginner musicians I met in Terlingua were every bit as nervous and self-conscious about performing as are beginners in any other part of the country. What makes Terlingua different, what allows it to be an incubator, is that the participatory spirit of music making—thinking about music as a social activity, rather than simply as a means of entertaining an audience—ultimately overrides concerns about talent and ability when it comes to determining who is encouraged to perform. As I learned, the roots of this spirit can be found in the earliest years of Terlingua's history, and in the unique social climate that was created there.

WHY TERLINGUA?

Terlingua's long tradition of amateur music making is due in part to the town's isolation and tiny population. In the early years of Terlingua's rebirth, a person had to be especially self-sufficient to live in the lower Big Bend, and a broad do-it-yourself mentality was born as a result. If you needed a place to live, you built your own house. If your vehicle needed maintenance, you learned the basics of auto mechanics. If you wanted entertainment, you created it yourself. There was simply no one else around to do these things for you.

When the first river guides began moving into the Terlingua Ghost Town in the late 1970s, opportunities for listening to music were fewer and farther between than almost anywhere else in the contiguous United States. AM radio was unreliable, FM radio was nonexistent, and the limited electric grid meant that playing pre-recorded music was not possible in all situations.[17] Gigging musicians rarely traveled to Terlingua in the town's first few decades because there was hardly anywhere in South Brewster County to play. This

scarcity of live and recorded music meant that early Terlinguans had something significant in common with their
nineteenth-century predecessors: if they wanted to hear music, they were going to have to create it themselves. Terlingua music was thus borne out of necessity as one of the only
means of entertainment for local residents to enjoy after the
sun went down. Thanks to nightly campfire jams, music
gradually gained a central role in Terlingua's daily life—a
role it has enjoyed ever since.

Today, the steadily growing population and infrastructure
have changed the game significantly, and the independence
of spirit that was once an essential part of life in the Big
Bend is now less of a necessity. Nevertheless, the DIY mentality that was born during those early years has remained
an important part of Terlingua's character and a powerful
driving force in the town's social and creative life. There are
local construction crews for hire now, but many Terlinguans
still choose to build their own homes, often despite a lack
of knowledge or prior experience. In previous decades, they
did this out of necessity. Today, they do it because they can
(significantly, the absence of building codes in South Brewster County helps make this possible). In Terlingua, you do
not have to be a brilliant author to write your own book; you
do not have to be a professional photographer or painter to
create works of art; you do not have to be a rock star to write
songs or record an album or perform your music in front of
an audience. It is the preservation of this attitude, developed
around campfires all those years ago, that allows Terlingua
to be so highly musical.

Of course, it is no guarantee that such an attitude should
be preserved once its reason for existing has expired. These
days, there is no shortage of good music and good musicians
in Terlingua, and providing space for all comers is no longer
a necessity to keep the music going. In order for amateurs to
continue to receive the opportunities they have long enjoyed
in the Terlingua music scene, local musicians must buy in to

the belief that there is value in supporting the contributions of less experienced performers. Ultimately, it is here that the most important piece of the puzzle comes into play. Above all else, it is a deep sense of community that allows Terlingua to be such a good incubator of music and musicians.

This kind of community will likely be familiar to residents of other small towns. It is a feeling of interconnectedness, of togetherness, one that is predicated on daily face-to-face interactions among neighbors who know each other and are invested in each other's lives. "It's kind of like a family. A big, dreaded family," one resident told me.

Carol Whitney agreed. "Back in civilization, it takes you months to get to know people," she said. "Even *years* sometimes if you move to a new place. But with the social scene on the Porch, with everybody getting together every day, you see these people all the time, and the curve of getting to know them is hugely accelerated. It's like Mayberry on acid."

Of all the reasons that people cite for choosing to live in Terlingua, the spirit of community is the most cherished. Practically everyone in town has a story about when they felt it first. Blues guitarist Pat O'Bryan moved to Terlingua a few months before my arrival. Writing on his blog, he recounted the day he drove to town with all his possessions to move into his new house. At the time, he had met only a smattering of people in Terlingua, and one of them called Pat to ask if he needed help unloading the moving van. "When we got there," Pat wrote, "there was a crowd of friends and neighbors waiting. Some of them were people I knew pretty well. Some I had met. One guy I'd never seen before. In very short order, the storage building was full and all the boxes we wanted in the house were in the house. After the work was done, we all met up at the [American] Legion and I basically bought the bar for the night. It was a great welcome to the neighborhood."

Part of the reason that this community spirit runs so deep in Terlingua is that no one lives there by accident. With very few exceptions, the people who live in Terlingua do so because they *want* to live in Terlingua. Only a handful of residents in the adult population were actually born in South Brewster County. All the rest have moved in from somewhere else. Furthermore, with the exception of seasonal river guides and a handful of state and national park employees, hardly anyone moves to Terlingua for a job—there simply aren't many jobs to be had, and those that are available typically don't pay well. Most Terlinguans view employment not as an opportunity to follow a particular professional calling, but rather as the necessary means for making a life in the desert possible. For these people, an overall sense of happiness and satisfaction is determined more by the place they're living than by the work they're doing. It is the singular experience of living in Terlingua, rather than finding a fulfilling career, that draws many residents to this unlikely place.

"That's the thing that we have in common in Terlingua," said Collie Ryan, a songwriter and painter who has lived in South Brewster County since 1980. "Whether we're rednecks arming for the future, or we're Christians or we're drunks or just real straight ordinary people, the one thing we all have in common is that we want to be here."

Pat O'Bryan agreed. "I think Terlingua is more of a *community* than anywhere I've ever lived," he said. "I mean, there's nobody here for a job, there's nobody here to go to school. I have friends living in tents, shacks, houses with no running water. If you're livin' down here it's 'cause you *want* to live down here."

It did not take long before I too began to feel this spirit of community. When I first arrived, a few people I met were admittedly skeptical about my motives; one local musician listened politely to my proposals about researching the Terlingua music scene before wondering aloud if I was going to be studying them "like bugs in a jar." My participation in the local music scene seemed to put most minds at ease, however, and once I was accepted into the fold, I felt more welcomed than I have ever been in a new place. It wasn't just that people were being cordial or polite. This seemed more intentional, more deliberate. It felt like people actually *wanted* me there.

Like many Terlingua residents, I was in town on a seasonal basis. For five years, I was in and out of the Big Bend—a little more than two years total time when everything was said and done. Leaving Terlingua on a regular basis served only to heighten my appreciation for the town's unique social climate. I grew to miss Terlingua each summer—how drivers wave as they pass each other on the highway; how I could go to the grocery store, the laundromat, or just about anywhere else in town and know that I would run into at least one friend; how every bar in town felt like my "home" bar, every gig my "home" venue. That deep sense of place is the kind of thing that makes you feel like you truly belong.

The more I experienced this community spirit, the more I began to realize that it was precisely this feeling, more than any other contributing factor, that was the driving force behind the high levels of musical participation in Terlingua. In our current age of musical specialization, when the overwhelming majority of the music we hear is created for us by professionals, very few people would be willing to sit and listen to a total stranger who is just beginning to learn how to perform. But when everyone on the Porch or on the stage is a neighbor or a friend, it becomes a lot easier to accept their musical contributions, regardless of ability.

This was precisely the spirit that drew Carol Whitney to Terlingua. "It's just small, and everybody knows everybody," she told me. "It's like how nobody gives a shit if you pull up in a Mercedes or not. Here, nobody gives a shit if you have a $5,000 Taylor guitar. It's that whole mental attitude of 'We accept everybody,' *especially* if you're more toward the bottom of the ladder. And that extends to the musicians, too. If you want to come up here and do your stuff, we're gonna give you a good listen. There's no bar set up that says *only if you meet this criteria can you participate in this community.* The criteria tend to be more about what kind of human being you are as opposed to whether you can play the best riff on a guitar or not."

Ultimately, my experience making music is what allowed me to fully understand and appreciate the spirit of community in Terlingua. At its heart, community isn't just about recognizing each other in the grocery store, waving at each other on the highway, or even about socializing with each other on a daily basis. It is more about *accepting* each other for who we are, about recognizing the common humanity in every person and celebrating the inherent worth that humanity bestows. It is about looking at another person and saying *I see you. I hear you.* That, in the end, is what music and community in Terlingua are all about.

None of this is to say that Terlingua is perfect, of course. Despite the town's undeniable success at encouraging musical participation, Terlingua is no utopia, musically or otherwise. Although the spirit of community shapes virtually every aspect of social life, the egalitarian ideal that is so clearly strived for is rarely (if ever) perfectly realized. For one thing, Carol Whitney was not entirely accurate when she suggested that the attitude, "You can't play with us because you're not good enough," is nonexistent in Terlingua. On the contrary, there have been musicians dating back to the earliest campfires who have been unenthusiastic about making music with their less skilled neighbors. While I witnessed numerous examples of beginners being encouraged in Terlingua, I also spoke with inexperienced musicians who said they felt unappreciated or even ignored whenever they attempted to participate in a local jam. Even on the Porch, people sometimes report feeling alienated rather than welcomed.

One of the most significant barriers to greater musical participation is the noticeable lack of gender parity in the Terlingua music scene. Although the town is home to a number of accomplished female musicians, musical events are often dominated by male participants, and this leaves a lot of women feeling that their contributions to the town's musical life are consistently undervalued. More than one such person referred to the Porch as a "boys' club" when I asked them why they did not attend more jams. Not every female musician in Terlingua feels this way—in fact, several women I spoke with roundly rejected the notion that gender plays any significant role in the Terlingua music scene. For others, however, this lack of gender diversity prevents many women from participating more actively in the town's musical life.

"All I know is that there's a shitload of girl musicians in Terlingua who don't come out and play very often," said violist Charlotte Teer. "And that's a downright cryin' shame."

A number of women I spoke with were quick to suggest that this gender gap is not an intentional creation of their male counterparts. "I don't think it's a deliberate exclusion of women," said June Rapp. "And I don't think it's that women are not being given opportunities. No one's gonna say, 'Girl, you can't play guitar.' I think if you want in, you gotta get in there and just *do* it."

Singer-songwriter Hillie Bills agreed. "I can only speak for myself," she wrote during a Facebook conversation about female musicians in Terlingua, "but I'm hesitant to invite myself into anything. It seems like men are better at doing that. I was just speaking to Kathy yesterday about all the incredibly strong women out here in particular who can really hold their own and then some. At the same time, I think even the strongest of women can be intimidated by things that many men don't realize are even factors. Just as I'm sure that a gaggle of women can send a man headed for the hills!"

Intentional or not, the barriers to participation for female musicians in Terlingua have inspired a number of local women to create their own opportunities for music making in hopes of encouraging more women to participate. This was Bryn Moore's motivation for organizing the Terlingua Gals Music Review, an annual event that began in 2016 and exclusively features local female artists. The Review was created in response to another Terlingua music showcase that had taken place earlier that year, an invite-only event that featured a long list of local songwriters. Tellingly, not a single female artist was invited to participate.

"That just may be part of why we decided to have our own thing," said Bryn Moore with a wry grin. "My dad once told me he thought I was a hold-my-beer-and-watch-this kind of girl. We took that to heart and decided that the girls needed to do their own thing. We never dreamt that it would be as exciting as it was for people. We had such a crowd the waitresses couldn't deliver the food to the tables. It was a turnout like we never expected." In the years since, the Terlingua Gals Music Review has become a highlight of the town's annual music calendar, featuring performers from five decades of Terlingua history and drawing crowds of local residents who are otherwise not active participants in Terlingua's musical life.

Bryn's Terlingua Gals Music Review was not the first attempt to create some gender parity in the local music scene. During my time in Terlingua, local painter and songwriter Collie Ryan also sought to address what she felt was a shortage of opportunities for female musicians when she began hosting regular song circles at the High Sierra, some of which are reserved exclusively for women. Collie's circles fill a unique niche in the Terlingua music scene: unlike open mics, they are held outside without the aid of amplifying equipment, and unlike Porch jams, where participants often play all at once, song circles emphasize taking turns performing solo and listening to others do the same.

"I like the idea of the open circle, 'cause it allows the men and women balance to happen better," said Collie. "Because when men get going with their music, it sort of marginalizes the women. And it's good and it's beautiful, but it's like, 'Okay, now we're gonna stop the freight train and do this real sweet ballad?' *Not*. Because the adrenaline is rolling and it must keep rolling like a freight train. I guess it's a man thing. And it's cool, it's great. But there could be a woman sitting there, and they're not necessarily gonna pass the energy to her to break that rhythm. Are you gonna stop the freight train rolling along at ninety miles an hour for Bryn to sing a song? Or me? That's what's so nice about the circle. There's more room for women."[18]

The aforementioned song circles at La Kiva, hosted by June Rapp and Mary Diesel, have had a similar effect. Although providing a space for female participants was not the organizers' explicit purpose, the overwhelming majority of the attendees are, in fact, women. Further, more than three-quarters of the participants at the circles I attended were people I had never heard perform at any other musical events in Terlingua. This supports what Charlotte suggested above: that there are a lot of women in Terlingua who, if provided the opportunity, would participate much more regularly in the town's musical life.

The gender disparity in the Terlingua music scene is not a new phenomenon. Notably, while many of the male musicians who arrived in Terlingua in the early decades of its rebirth describe being welcomed into the fold almost immediately, women who arrived at the same time often recount the opposite experience. "You didn't get a lot of respect in Terlingua from the guy musicians," recalled Chris Muller, who moved to Terlingua in the early 1980s. "The audiences, they were wonderful. And it wasn't all of the men all of the time, but there were a lot of them that just . . . there was not a lot of respect."

Charlotte Teer, who has been living and performing in Terlingua since the late 1970s, agreed. "At campfires, we held our own," she said, "but for gigs we needed a way in. It was really a boys club sort of thing. The guys just would *not* have us. That was the inspiration for Just Us Girls, and our twice-a-week gigs at the Starlight Theatre for two years."

Just Us Girls is among the most esteemed bands in Terlingua's long musical history. Active through most of the 1990s, the group was an all-female quintet that featured Charlotte on viola, Chris Muller on guitar, Chris Baker on flute and guitar, Shanna Cowell on bass, and Evie Dorsey on classical guitar, percussion, and kazoo. They recorded a cassette during their tenure, and they performed numerous gigs all over South Brewster County and the greater Big Bend region, even opening for the Dixie Chicks when they visited the Big Bend.

According to the band members, Terlingua's male-dominated music scene provided the impetus they needed for starting their own band. "When I got there, it was only men," said Evie Dorsey. She recounted an experience that had been shared by several female musicians in Terlingua. A local all-male band would book a gig at a venue in town and then invite a woman to join them during their performance. "And so they'd say to the women, 'Bring your guitar, you can sit in.' And we'd sit there all night, trying not to drink too much so we could remember the words if we ever got a turn. And they would never ask us to sit in. Finally I said, 'Girls, this is absurd. We can do what they can do, only doin' what *we* do. We're gonna make music. And if the guys won't let us play, heck, we'll start our own band. We'll call it Just Us Girls—JUGS for short.'"

The continuing lack of gender parity in the town's music scene reveals an important lesson. Despite its deeply held convictions, its emphasis on community, and its calls for a more egalitarian social and musical order, Terlingua is not immune to the broader societal ills of the nation. This is something that Terlingua women know firsthand. "Terlingua doesn't exist free of the influences of the United States and the historical cultural moment," said Evie Dorsey.

Members of Just Us Girls perform on the Starlight Theatre main stage, 2018.
From left: Tim Callahan, Charlotte Teer, Chris Baker, Shanna Cowell.

Mary Diesel agrees. "We aren't making the assumption that the issues that happen in the other parts of our culture don't happen here, in terms of discrimination and exclusion or whatever you want to call it. It's *so* ingrained in our culture." Mary referenced a Facebook conversation in which a local man opined that "social sexual stereotypes don't apply south of the Border Patrol checkpoint" (located sixty miles north of Terlingua). While it was easy to appreciate the spirit in which the remark was made, Mary pointed out that such statements actually serve to whitewash Terlinguan social life by rendering invisible its very real shortcomings. "Reading that conversation," she said, "it kind of gives you the idea that *Oh, no, that doesn't happen here.* Like we're beyond that. But it's part of our culture that is broader than Terlingua. We have to be paying attention in Terlingua, and some of us are more than others."

Obviously, Terlingua is far from perfect. This acknowl-
edgment, however, should not obscure the fact that when it
comes to providing opportunities for musical participation,
the town is doing a lot of things right. After all, many of the
women quoted here also credit Terlingua's unique social climate for their growth as musicians, even as they recognize
that their community still has a long way to go before the
process of music making is fully democratized. Whether or
not that democratization takes place is ultimately up to Terlinguans themselves.

MY TWO YEARS in Terlingua fundamentally changed how
I think about music. Fresh off eight years of music school, I
had been steeped in the traditional training grounds for the
professional musical class, an environment where "talent"
is king and ability of the utmost concern. Terlingua gave me
a view of what is possible when other considerations take
center stage—when the "magical world of the musicians"
is democratized, rather than exclusive and hierarchical, and
when the process of music making is valued for its own sake,
rather than simply being the means to an end. I was regularly moved by the experiences of people like Carol, who
had been a closet player for years before ever working up
the courage to perform in public, and of people like Ed, who
likely would never have realized his dream of learning the
dulcimer had it not been for the encouragement of the Terlingua community. I looked at them and thought of other
people I knew, others whose lifelong passion for music had
never been allowed to blossom simply because it had never
been nurtured. I recalled friends from my days in high school
band, many of whom had given up music after graduation
thanks to a lack of encouragement or a lack of opportunity.
How many of them might still be musically active if they
lived in a place like Terlingua?

Of course, my perspective was shaped by the fact that I
had only recently arrived in town. Even while I was busy

viewing my new surroundings with a sense of transformative awe, others were worried that Terlingua's days as a musical incubator were coming to an end. "These days I vacillate between being inspired and being intimidated," said Bryn Moore. A painter and singer-songwriter who has lived in Terlingua since 1985, Bryn has seen the music scene grow tremendously since she first arrived in town, both in the number of participants and in overall ability. "There's so many good musicians here now, and I am almost always intimidated when there's a group playing. I don't have that much experience playing with other people, and there can be . . . expectations there."

Others agreed. "There was a time when the Porch just felt a little bit more equal," said June Rapp not long after I met her for the first time in Ted's recording studio. "I just don't get that feeling now." June recalled that when she moved to Terlingua in the early 1990s, musicians on the Porch actively encouraged her to join them and to perform her own songs. Now, she told me, it just feels competitive. "There's just a lot of energy goin' on there now. If I were to take my guitar up to the Porch, I wouldn't be heard."

These comments caught me off guard at first because they did not match my own experience. However, the more time I spent in Terlingua, the more I began to notice a disjuncture between the way new arrivals like myself viewed the music scene and the way it was perceived by longtime Terlingua residents. I had arrived in the Big Bend at a transitional moment in the town's history, a time when Terlingua was just beginning to develop a broader reputation for music. No longer an afterthought in the world of Texas music, Terlingua was becoming a destination. Some, like Carol, had come looking for a community-oriented approach to music making. Others, especially performers from musically saturated cities like Dallas and Austin, saw Terlingua as a promised land of abundant paying gigs and relatively little competition. This newfound notoriety has brought more musicians to Terlingua than ever. For the listening public, the quality and variety of music now on display in Terlingua is as good as it has ever been. But many of these newcomers arrive in town with their own understandings about the meanings of musical performance, often completely unaware that Terlingua has a long history of doing things its own way. For musicians who have spent years living and making music in Terlingua, the result of these changing dynamics is palpable.

I recall witnessing one particular event that demonstrated this to me. It was a Sunday afternoon and a handful of high-caliber musicians were visiting from out of town. They were joined on the Porch by some of the more experienced local musicians, and as the day progressed, the music grew into a raucous jam with as many as ten people playing at once. The jam was in full swing when I arrived, and it was already crowded enough that squeezing in would have been difficult. Rather than attempting to join, I left my guitar in its case under one of the Porch benches, grabbed a folding chair, and took a seat just outside the circle of musicians to listen.

Before long, a local violinist named Jane arrived and sat down next to me. Jane has been playing the violin since childhood, but she was still learning how to play by ear. Jane took out her violin and waited. The group was blazing through a fast song, and when it ended, they immediately jumped into another, followed again by another. After three or four songs, Jane leaned over to me and spoke into my ear.

"I don't think I can play along with any of these songs," she confessed. After perhaps ten more minutes of sitting, Jane put her violin back in its case, having never played a note. As she was standing up to leave, the group wrapped up a song and one of the participants looked up at her.

"Do you have a song, Jane?" he asked. Jane quietly declined and the music continued. At the time, I interpreted the invitation as a gesture of welcome. But looking back on that day, I realize that the reality was a bit more complicated.

Jane was just beginning to learn how to participate in such an event, so she was not in the position to lead the group in a song. If the musicians had truly wanted Jane to participate, they would have slowed down and played some songs that were easier for someone new to jamming to follow. Instead, when Jane declined to lead a song, the other musicians turned back inward and launched into yet another barn burner. While their gesture may have been intended as a friendly invitation, in the context of the moment, it seemed much more intimidating than welcoming.

Whenever longtime Terlingua musicians tell me that their music scene feels less inclusive than it used to, these are the kinds of examples they cite. Some wonder aloud if this is perhaps inevitable as Terlingua continues to grow. With more musicians in town, venues can afford to be choosier in hiring performers, while musicians on the Porch—some of them likely unaware of the long history of community-oriented music in Terlingua—might be tempted to shun less experienced performers in favor of the better players sitting next to them, just as they would be expected to do in almost any other town in the United States.

Ultimately, being a music incubator is something that can only happen by choice. When a community of musicians chooses to encourage less experienced musicians to participate, it creates opportunities for people like Ed and Carol to have the transformative experiences they described. Of course, this can and does lead to performances that are of lower musical "quality," and this is a trade-off that most musicians in most other music scenes are unwilling to make. This is one reason why a small town like Terlingua has a big advantage when it comes to being an incubator—put simply, it is easier to accept the contributions of less skilled musicians when those musicians are friends and neighbors rather than strangers.

This final observation weighed on me as I sat with Carol in front of her trailer beneath the cottonwood tree. I asked her about it as we packed up our guitars for the evening. "What do you think will happen to the music scene as Terlingua continues to grow?"

"I don't know," Carol replied. "I fear that it may become one of those deals where the bar kind of keeps getting set higher and higher, until after a while it'll only be, you know, kind of like a Nashville. *If you're not at this caliber, we don't want you.* Right now, just about anybody can show up and they'll be welcomed and accepted. That's why it's an incubator of music. And once the incubation is done and the egg is hatched, that incubator might go away. I hope it doesn't. I hope it doesn't become a place where you go to compete to play the best music. But I can see it happening. We're starting to get a lot more, you know, the Austinites and the Kervillites coming down here." I had heard this concern expressed by others in town as well: that control of the Terlingua music scene might be wrested from local musicians as more and more visiting performers continue to arrive from out of town.

"So far during my time here, it hasn't seemed to get a whole lot worse . . . or better. You know, however you want to look at it." Carol let out a laugh and the tension eased for a moment. "I don't see it changing drastically. I fear that it might, but time will tell. What happens here, that never happens anywhere else. And I hope it stays this way. I'm afraid it may not, but I hope it does. And I'm going to do my best to encourage it to stay this way."

CHAPTER 3

THE AUSTIN EFFECT

Things weren't working out in the city
So I moved out to the prairie

Here in the country things are simple
People follow through with what they say they'll do

I found a job building my home
It ain't hard, it's just dirt and stone

My friends and family, they say they'll visit me here
I'm still waiting, it's been a year

It ain't their fault, they're stuck in the city
They're paying off their homes, paying off loans

As for me, I ain't wastin' time
That's why I'm singing and working on my rhymes
Working on something I can leave behind

When I die the dogs will scatter my bones
And there I'll lie amongst the dirt and stones
—TREVOR REICHMAN, "Dirt and Stone"[1]

BUILDING WITH ADOBE is a simple but time-consuming process. It begins with dirt, the ideal ratio being roughly two parts sand to one part clay. Many Terlinguans are lucky to have just the right mixture occurring naturally on their property, often only feet from their front doors, allowing them to dig it directly from the ground and begin building. The second ingredient in adobe is a fibrous binding agent that holds the prepared mixture together. Straw, the most common choice, is not easy to come by in South Brewster County. Fortunately, the tall and wispy grasses that can be found growing in abundance throughout the Big Bend also work well. The third and final ingredient is water, the most difficult of the three to procure in Terlingua. Since rain collection is the most popular local method for obtaining water (wells here are prohibitively expensive and frequently unreliable), many Terlinguans choose to build their houses in reverse order: first comes a metal roof supported at the corners, followed by the gutters and cisterns of the water catchment system. After waiting for six months to a year for the tanks to fill, the long and laborious process of mixing and forming the adobe can finally begin. It takes a lot of patience to build a house this way, but when the walls finally begin to take shape, all the main ingredients are free.

Trevor Reichman built his home in this manner, and the process took him almost nine years to complete. His house is a simple structure, a circular earthen dome measuring about ten feet tall and eighteen feet in diameter. With its smooth lines and lime plaster, the "Dome" looks like something out of *Star Wars*, its beiges and tans blending seamlessly into its stark desert surroundings. Trevor constructed his one-room home almost entirely without the aid of power tools or heavy construction equipment. Grass was harvested with a machete; dirt was excavated with pick and shovel and sifted using a piece of diamond lath fastened over a simple wooden frame; the mixing was done with bare hands and feet on a large canvas tarp. The walls were raised slowly and deliberately, one mudpie at a time.

Trevor does not possess a contractor's license, and he had no previous construction experience when he began working on the Dome. A house like his would be illegal in most parts

Terlingua Ranch, with Nine Point Mesa in the background, 2016.

of the United States, but in Terlingua there are no building codes, so there is practically no limit to what can be built or who can build it. "You start off with a low standard of living compared to what you might be used to," Trevor admitted with a wry smile, recalling how he slept in his car during the early part of the construction process. "But the cost of living is low, too, so it's kind of a blank slate to build what you want. Anything is possible."

Trevor's property is located on Terlingua Ranch, a vast sprawling area off Texas Highway 118 about twenty miles northeast of the Ghost Town. It would not be inaccurate to think of the Ranch as a kind of "suburb" of Terlingua, but such terms can give a misleading image of the area's population density, considering that even the closest neighbors can be more than a quarter mile apart.

Trevor is an energetic spokesperson for his unconventional off-grid existence, but he does not come across as preachy or sanctimonious, as people with similar lifestyles sometimes do. Instead, he is soft-spoken, thoughtful, and deliberate, with an even temperament not prone to excessive highs or lows. When welcoming visitors, he guides them around his twenty-acre homestead with an understated yet palpable enthusiasm. He points out a clothesline he has strung among the creosote bushes and a fenced-in garden where he grows tomatoes, kale, chard, squash, lettuce, cantaloupe, beets, eggplant, and spinach. A young cottonwood tree next to the Dome survives on the gray water from his kitchen sink. A 550-gallon cistern collects rainwater from the roof of a nearby prefabricated shed that doubles as a guest house, while a second storage shed is topped with 800 watts of solar panels, Trevor's only source of electricity. A hand-built wooden outhouse contains a bucket-style composting toilet, and an outdoor shower provides spectacular views of the nearby Christmas Mountains to the south. Interspersed throughout these modest developments are the native flora and fauna of the Chihuahuan Desert, the boundaries between the "human" and the "natural" left intentionally vague.

As his song "Dirt and Stone" suggests, Trevor moved to the Big Bend after years living in the city. Following a decade in Austin, he moved to Portland to take a desk job with the online music distributor CD Baby—"on the other side of the music industry," he observed with a grin. In 2008, he was in the process of returning to Austin to pursue a full-time career as a singer-songwriter when he made a spontaneous trip to the Big Bend. Like so many others before him, Trevor was hooked. "It was cheap land," he recalled, "and it seemed like a blank slate, like anything was possible. I instantly loved the community and felt like almost everyone I became friends with or met was genuinely interested in helping me get started."

An environmentalist at heart, Trevor had long cultivated an interest in sustainable off-grid living, and seeing the possibilities for that enterprise in South Brewster County convinced him to buy land on Terlingua Ranch and start

Trevor Reichman in the Dome, 2016.

from scratch. "As soon as I bought the land, there was a lot of synchronicity," he said. "A neighbor down the road offered to help me start a structure. And then I started getting gigs around the area, paid gigs. Whereas, comparing that to a place like Austin, which has a really high cost of living and is already very musically saturated, it seemed like . . . I thought I would just stick around here and see what came of it, see where it led. And I'm still here."

When hearing Trevor's story for the first time, most people will likely assume that by moving to Terlingua, he must have effectively abandoned his pursuit of a music career. As it turns out, the opposite is true: since his arrival in 2008, Trevor has made his living almost entirely from music. "That's the thing about small towns," he told me. "If there's something that's not being provided, and you want to provide that, there's a place for you. Whereas in a city, there could be too many others already doing what you want to do for a living. It amazes me how many musicians still flock to

those places. If you're a doctor, you wouldn't want to move
to a city where it's mostly doctors and not enough patients.
It's just not as obvious for some reason with the creative
arts."

For someone who earns most of his income from live performance, Trevor's choice to move to a tiny, remote desert
town, rather than to an established music capital, seems to
defy every shred of conventional wisdom. However, Trevor
is adamant that his unorthodox path to a music career is
more sensible than it might at first appear. He is not alone.
Although music has always been a casual pursuit for most
local musicians, Terlingua has a long history of professional
music—that is to say, of musicians (particularly songwriters)
who earn a majority of their income from musical endeavors.

Of all the myriad insights I gained during my time in
the Big Bend, this was perhaps the most surprising. I had
always assumed that moving to an urban area with a well-
known music scene was practically a necessity for anyone
attempting to make a living as a performer. Indeed, for the
vast majority of professional musicians this thinking is still
considered common sense. But as I got to know more and
more people in Terlingua—including a number of musicians
who had fled Austin in exchange for a life in the desert—
I gradually began to realize that my assumptions about life
in our nation's musical capitals were fundamentally flawed.
After all, I had been operating from an outsider's perspective;
I had never actually attempted to earn a living as a musician
in any of those places. The more I heard from people who
had experienced them for themselves, the more I began to
see the wisdom in Trevor's thinking.

Ultimately, musicians choose to move to Terlingua for
many of the same reasons that attract other residents. For
those pursuing careers in music, however, the benefits of
remote desert life often prove particularly—and unexpectedly—advantageous. By challenging the notion that living
in the city is a prerequisite for professional musicians, these

intrepid performers are forging new paths to successful music careers at a time when many of the most renowned music centers in the United States are dealing with crises of gentrification, population growth, and skyrocketing costs of living. Just look at Austin.

"THE LIVE MUSIC CAPITAL OF THE WORLD"

As an aspiring musician growing up in the oilfields of West Texas, I always considered one thing to be gospel: if you wanted to "make it" as a musician in Texas, you had to go to Austin. Such thinking makes sense. The state capital has the biggest reputation for music of any city in the state, and it is home to one of the largest and most lucrative music scenes in the nation, bringing in hundreds of millions of dollars in annual revenue. "In the notoriously bicoastal entertainment and multimedia worlds," wrote Christopher Gray in the *Austin Chronicle* in 2011, "it's the only city in Texas that matters to both the taste-making class of music bloggers and hardwired establishment bodies such as the Recording Academy—i.e., the people who give out the Grammys."[2]

Compared to cities like New York, Los Angeles, Nashville, and Detroit, Austin is a relative newcomer in the nation's musical consciousness, beginning its meteoric rise from afterthought to industry center as recently as 1970. In August of that year, the legendary Armadillo World Headquarters opened for business, and it soon became Austin's first nationally renowned performance venue, attracting numerous A-list acts that not long before would have spurned Austin in favor of larger nearby cities such as Dallas, Houston, and San Antonio. At around the same time, a handful of Texas natives who had achieved success in the major music industry centers, led by Willie Nelson and Michael Murphey, began settling in Austin. Thanks in large part to their influence, and shaped by Austin's status as a liberal island within a politically conservative state, Austin-area musicians began to develop their own distinctive sound and associated style. Hard-edged, gritty, and inspired by the folk music revival of the previous decade, what became known as "progressive country" combined signifiers of the redneck with those of the hippie, thus fashioning an identity out of an oxymoron—the so-called cosmic cowboy—while reinventing country music for a generation of young Texans who grew up amid the counterculture of the 1960s and 70s.

In his book *The Improbable Rise of Redneck Rock*, Jan Reid recounted how Austin's newfound musical identity gained immediate national exposure for the city. "Soon Austin was swarming with talented young musicians," he wrote, "and the most popular public spectacle was now live music. Through a curious national press and word-of-mouth communication by touring musicians, Austin gained almost overnight a reputation as one of the most exciting centers of musical activity in the country."[3]

For Austin-area musicians, life was good. Although few people were getting rich playing music in Austin, the combination of ample gigging opportunities and a low cost of living made Austin an ideal climate for pursuing music full-time. "It goes without saying that there was next to no money to be made by musicians," wrote Bill Bentley in the *Austin Chronicle*, "but in the early Seventies, it was still possible to live in Austin on almost nothing but air. . . . It's hard to imagine now, but Austin had produced an incredible ecosystem where musicians found places to play and plentiful audiences to play for, without much more of a support system than a few music stores and gas stations to get a dollar's worth of ethyl."[4]

When hearing accounts of 1970s Austin, it is hard to miss their uncanny resemblance to present-day descriptions of Terlingua. "[Austin is] the only place I know where people sit around for hours and talk about how great it is to live here," said Jim Franklin, one of the Armadillo's founders.[5] In his book *Cosmic Cowboys and New Hicks*, Travis Stimeling writes that musicians flocked to the state capital in the 1970s in part because of its "small-town atmosphere." Chet Flippo, writing in *Texas Parade* in 1974, observed that Austin musicians enjoyed a "strong sense of community and group identity" and also that "the [Texas] Hill Country is a most desirable place to live. Every one of the major singers who migrated here has, at one time or another, lived in the traditional music capitals but they gave it all up for the hills and lakes. Who can blame them?"[6] In the same article, Flippo, who eventually became the Austin correspondent for *Rolling Stone*, listed a number of musicians who fled to Austin from the coastal music capitals, many of whom—Nelson, Murphey, Asleep at the Wheel, Doug Sahm, and Jerry Jeff Walker among them—would eventually become Austin music icons. According to Flippo, these musicians chose Austin because they felt like "misfits" in L.A. or Nashville, and because they wanted a "simpler life" in a smaller city. "The Hill Country renegades," he wrote, "prefer a lower-keyed life in a stone house or log cabin by a lake to a ragged life in a series of motel rooms. They're ready to trade—and most have traded—a certain amount of income for a measure of musical integrity and freedom. The Austin area offers them, first of all, a place to lead a comfortable, low-pressure life. They further have the advantages of being in a community of like-minded individuals, where there is a built-in audience and club circuit unmatchable anywhere. For many, it's the ideal life."[7]

Austin did not receive its trademark moniker until 1991, when the city council voted to adopt the slogan "Live Music Capital of the World" after an Austin Music Commission study noted that the city possessed an unusually large number of live music venues per capita. Several decades later, the effects of this brilliant marketing strategy are still being felt. While plenty of other Texas cities enjoy flourishing music scenes of their own (Houston, Dallas, San Antonio, Denton, and Lubbock come immediately to mind), Austin's centrality within the wider world of Texas music is undeniable. Annual festivals like South by Southwest and Austin City Limits have become global brands that attract hundreds of thousands of visitors to the city each year. Significantly, many of the people who attend these festivals have no other entry point into the rich tradition of Texas music. Put simply, no other place has been more effective in branding itself as the state's musical nucleus or in broadcasting this image to the wider world. As a result, Austin's status as the unchallenged music capital of Texas has made it the default reference point for thinking about Texas music. It is little wonder that so many kids like me grew up assuming that Austin was the only logical place in the state to pursue a music career.

While musicians with Austin connections are scattered throughout the state, Terlingua's ties to Austin are stronger than most. The overwhelming majority of its resident musicians lived and performed in the state capital—some of them for decades—before relocating to the Big Bend. Among them is guitarist and songwriter Bruce Salmon, who moved to Austin in 1980 to pursue a career as a professional musician, remaining there for thirty-four years before relocating to the Terlingua area in 2014. Bruce recalls that Austin in the 1980s possessed all the qualities that made it an ideal destination for aspiring performers. "There was a lot of infrastructure support for music," he said. "The *Austin Chronicle* [a periodical covering local music] started right after I moved there, and not long after that was the first year of South by Southwest. Both were still small and went hand in hand with the local culture that had built up there, through the cosmic cowboys and the Armadillo and the punk rock scene. There was also a lot of really cheap rent back then, for venues and musicians. And it wasn't all that competitive. . . . Some clubs that are still open actually paid musicians more in 1985 than they do now, when my rent was sixty-five dollars and a beer was a dollar fifty. It's crazy."

IT IS IMPOSSIBLE TO SAY definitively just how long Austin's ideal musical climate lasted—or whether it is ongoing—as each person's perspective depends on when he or she arrived in the city. Musicians who moved to Austin in the 1980s have told me that paying gigs started to become scarce in the 1990s, and I have heard from musicians who moved to Austin in the mid-2000s that the 2010s have constituted the city's real turning point. Michael Murphey, one of the musicians most responsible for developing Austin's reputation, said in an interview in 1974 that the city was already "becoming too much of a scene" and that he was considering relocating to somewhere quieter.[8] "Scenes have destroyed an awful lot of places," Murphey told another reporter a year earlier. "I'd hate to see people with guitars on their backs suddenly showing up by the thousands. Because they're gonna starve." Steve Fromholz, another leading light of early Austin, agreed. "If the hype gets too bad," he said in 1973, "all the pickers I know will lay back and hide."[9] These words would prove prescient. Murphey left Austin in 1974, and Fromholz eventually moved to Terlingua.

Regardless of when they arrived, most current Austin musicians seem to agree that making a living as a musician in the state capital is becoming increasingly difficult with each passing year. Once spoken of in glowing terms as an almost utopian alternative to the coastal music capitals, Austin's music scene is now frequently described using words like "crisis" and "tipping point."

The Austin of the present bears little resemblance to the small city of the 1970s. The population of the Austin Metropolitan Area has exploded in the decades since the city began developing its musical reputation, surging from just under 400,000 in 1970 to more than 2 million by 2015, and nearly doubling in size since 2000. According to US Census data, Austin's population surged 20 percent from 2010 to 2016 alone, leading the *Austin American-Statesman* to report in 2019 that Austin is "the fastest growing large metropolitan area in the country for eight years running." Not surprisingly, the influx of new residents has led to a housing shortage, which has been further exacerbated in recent years by the growing popularity of websites such as VRBO.com and Airbnb.com, and the associated conversion of long-term rentals that were once inhabited by permanent residents into more lucrative short-term rentals for visitors. Real estate prices across the Austin Metropolitan Area, particularly in lower-income areas of the city, have skyrocketed as the housing shortage has become more pronounced.

Today, lamentations about Austin's growth, and the changes that growth has produced, have become as much a part of life in the city as the music. I have heard both current and past residents recount stories of low-rent neighborhoods being slowly bought up and converted into vacation rentals and chic housing, of quirky music venues and coffee shops being bulldozed to make room for hotels and cookie-cutter high-rises, of once-quiet local hangouts losing their charm as they are filled to the bursting point. The struggle for Austin's soul, as it were, is implicit in popular slogans like "Keep Austin Weird" and "Life's Too Short to Live in Dallas" and can be read in a legion of blog posts and newspaper and magazine articles concerning the city's rapid change.

In fact, concern over Austin's growth and changing social climate is such a common topic of discussion that *The Daily Show with Jon Stewart* parodied the outcries of Austin residents while broadcasting from the city in October 2014. In a pivot from the subject of immigration at the US-Mexico border, one of the show's correspondents said that "I am actually at where the *real* immigration crisis is: the Austin border. Austin's border with *everywhere else*. The human influx into this city is out of control and the locals are fucking *pissed.*" A second correspondent said, "Local Austinites are mad as hell. One native told me, and I quote, 'This is *not* the Austin I grew up in . . . when I moved here two years ago.'" The live studio audience cheered so loudly for this segment that the host temporarily broke character. "Wow," Stewart said with an astonished laugh. "The crowd really does seem hostile to people coming here. You know, when you write something, you don't really know if it's gonna hit a nerve. Boy, that's a fucking root canal we hit on that one."

While the changes that have accompanied Austin's rapid growth have affected every resident in one way or another, their impact has been especially pronounced on lower-income residents. This includes musicians and others employed in the arts, many of whom have long survived precariously at the bottom of the economic spectrum. A number of high-profile music venues have closed in recent years, among them Holy Mountain and Red 7 (closed in 2015 due to rent increases upward of 50 percent), the Austin Music Hall (closed in 2016 and converted to an office building), Strange Brew (closed in 2017 due to rent increases and "other financial factors"), and Threadgill's, one of the most iconic venues in Austin music history and the place where Janis Joplin famously got her start (both locations closed, one in 2018 due to rising rent and the other in April 2020 due to a combination of factors including increased property taxes and COVID-19 restrictions). A widely shared 2015 article on the music website *Pitchfork* argued that "the state of live music in [Austin] is currently at a tipping point," thus echoing the fears expressed by many Austin musicians. Focusing on the struggles of a handful of venues in Austin's Red River District, a designated cultural zone where a number of clubs are located, author David Sackllah observed, "Currently, that area, as well as many other musical aspects of the city, are in danger of losing ground to a combination of gentrification, big business, and city policies." It is a claim that rings true in the experiences of many Austin musicians. "We've seen a lot of really beautiful clubs meet their demise," one longtime local musician lamented in 2017. "It's harder and harder to find venues that can actually afford to rent dirt here in Austin, Texas."[10]

Further complicating the equation is the belief among both past and present Austin musicians that local artists have slowly been displaced in favor of better-known national and international artists as the city's musical reputation has grown. Nowhere is this more evident than in the PBS TV show-turned-festival Austin City Limits (ACL) and the annual South by Southwest (SXSW) festival. These events are easily the largest ambassadors for the Austin music scene today, collectively bringing 600,000 visitors and more than $600 million in annual revenue to the city. While it would be easy for an outside observer to see the success of these festivals and conclude that the state of professional music in Austin is healthy, longtime Austin musicians are quick to point out that these events bear scant resemblance to their earliest iterations. Both were founded during Austin music's earlier decades, and both were created with the intention of showcasing local talent.[11] However, as the popularity of these events has grown, the number of local performers in both has diminished significantly. During the first season of *Austin City Limits* in 1976, all but one of the performers were regulars on the Austin music circuit. During the 2017–2018 season, only two local artists were featured. Similarly, at the inaugural SXSW Festival in 1987, 130 of the 174 artists who performed were Austin musicians, amounting to almost 75 percent of the festival lineup. By comparison, of the 576 artists scheduled to perform at the 2018 festival, only 75—or 13 percent—were from Austin. For many observers, the symbolic culmination of this trend came in 2014, when Doritos paid Lady Gaga $2.5 million to perform an hour-long show at their SXSW showcase.

When confronted with these numbers, it seems that Austin musicians are justified in their complaints. It is a process of musical gentrification that parallels the broader process of gentrification in Austin: just as local residents are being increasingly displaced by new higher-income arrivals, so too are local artists being displaced from their hometown festivals. Of course, even as current Austin musicians continue their struggle to find profitable gigs, the city's ever-increasing prominence as a center for music has resulted in a continuing influx of new musicians into the city. With each passing year, a greater number of musicians are competing for a smaller number of paid performance opportunities. This begs the question as to whether Austin's ongoing campaign to market itself as the "Live Music Capital of the World" has perhaps been *too* successful; by attracting ever more musicians to the city, it has had the unintended consequence of making life more difficult for the very musicians on whom its reputation relies.

By 2015, the situation had become so dire that the City of Austin, in an attempt to address the crisis, commissioned an independent report on the state of the commercial music economy.[12] The results confirmed what most Austin musicians already knew. According to the survey, 81.2 percent of the almost 4,000 total respondents agreed that stagnating pay for musicians had an "extreme or strong impact" that made it "difficult to make a viable living," with half of all Austin musicians living below or just above the federal poverty line, and 60 percent of respondents working two or more jobs. In a particularly staggering figure for a self-proclaimed "Live Music Capital," nearly 70 percent of responding musicians said they earn less than $10,000 annually in music-related income. The report also confirmed anecdotal evidence that many venues "[pay] most local bands *less* than (or in the best case, the same as) they would have ten years ago." Venues are also struggling thanks to "expensive leases, high operating costs, short-term lease contracts, productivity losses from perceived regulatory inefficiencies, and declining 'cover' revenue."[13]

Crucially, the report took cost-of-living increases—including housing, food, and transportation—into account as well and concluded that these were also having a devastating effect on musicians. As of 2013, Austin had the highest average rent in Texas, and as a result, "Austinites trying to afford housing on minimum wage need to work close to three full-time jobs." Even including outside work, nearly one-third of Austin musicians earn below minimum wage. It is no wonder, then, that the report found "musicians are beginning to move out of Austin altogether due to the cumulative effect of affordability issues."

The Austin Music Census was discussed widely among musicians in both Terlingua and Austin. "They could've asked an Austin (or, more prevalently, an ex-Austin) musician any time in the last two decades and found out that Austin was way past its 'Live Music Capital of the World' days," wrote Terlingua musician and ex-Austinite Pat O'Bryan. "Austin became the Live Music Capital of the World—kinda—in the 70s and early 80s because you could rent a 3-bedroom home in South Austin for less than $400 a month. Gigs back then paid about what they pay now, so a musician could play two or three nights a week and the bills were paid. Pot was cheap. Gigs were plentiful, and included free beer, easy parking, and an educated, appreciative—although usually stoned—audience. There were more clubs per capita—commercial rent was cheap, too. I gave up on Austin when we tried very, very hard to stop Barton Creek Mall—and watched as the developers paid off the lawmakers and won that one. That was just one moment . . . one dot on the continuum . . . but, I left soon after. Now, the city's paid some consultants $45,000 to tell them something any guitar player could've told 'em for free. Except, I think they sugarcoated it."

It makes sense, when viewed in this context, why Trevor Reichman chose not to move to Austin to pursue music full-time. "I think Austin is a great music community," he told me, "but it's overly saturated, and the music business in Austin takes advantage of that saturation. So you have a great music community, but they're spending most of their time doing something else as a livelihood, instead of spending more time on their craft."

I admitted to Trevor that, as a kid growing up in Texas, Austin had always loomed large in my imagination, a mythical shining city on the hill where life as a musician was possible.

"It's odd," Trevor observed. "You look at a place like Terlingua, which is considered a poor town, or definitely not a wealthy town, and all the venues give a guarantee. And they know that it's important to treat the musicians well because they're a big part of the community, and that money just gets passed back around to the venues anyway. In Austin—which is a very wealthy town, and the city as a whole really gains a lot from the draw of the music—that money doesn't make its way back to the musicians. I find that odd. I find it odd that it's even legal, 'cause in what other profession can you not pay someone for a job done? Especially in a place that bills itself as the 'Live Music Capital of the World.' I call Austin the 'Music *Capitalists* of the World.' They capitalize off it. I try not to be bitter about it, but it has kind of formed my mindset that when I tour, I avoid proclaimed music scenes as much as possible. Instead, I try to look on the map for the little Terlinguas around the country."

MAÑANALAND

Many of the people who call Terlingua home once lived in Austin, and most ultimately fled the city due to its rapid growth. "It used to be that you could just zip to the usual places," said Sha Reed Gavin, who moved from Austin to

Terlingua in 2013. "But it got harder and harder to zip. When I first moved there, there was one stoplight between 360 and Cuernavaca. And then they put in a couple more. And I said, 'If they ever get to five stoplights, I'm gonna move closer to town.' And then they put more in, so that within the span of a month there were nine stoplights between 360 and Cuernavaca. I remember one night when we were trying to cross Barton Springs Road, and it took, like, twenty lights. And Jeff said, 'That's it. We're either staying home or we're moving.'"

When Terlingua residents describe what brought them to the desert, they often use their experience of cities as a foil, contrasting the trials of urban life (congestion, anonymity, hurried interactions) with what they consider to be the parallel advantages of small-town life (open spaces, community sentiment, slower pace). In fact, themes like these are such a common feature of Terlinguan discourse that they have become staples of the local songwriters' repertoire." I work a job in the city," sings longtime Terlingua resident Alice Knight in her song "Mañanaland":

> Always rushing around
> When I look into the mirror
> I see a perpetual frown
> Maybe I make more money
> But I just spend it faster
> So I'm leaving big city life behind me
> To be my own lord and master[14]

Trevor Reichman's song "Traffic," which was written specifically with Austin in mind, depicts his own exasperation with life in the nation's fastest growing metro area:

> What's the problem with the automobile
> Supposed to get you there faster up and over the hill
> If that's true then why do we spend
> Time trapped in this traffic for hours on end

What used to be a park is now a parking lot
Still there's no more place to park
I go downtown lookin' for a spot
The cars are circling around the block

(Chorus)
And there's traffic, traffic
Traffic, traffic

They say let's build another road
It's gonna ease the load
We all know
That the traffic's gonna follow where you go

(Chorus)

I'd rather take the train
Or a bicycle lane
It's drivin' me insane
When the traffic is on the road again

(Chorus)

Takes time from your day
About an hour each way
They say it's here to stay
But not me, I'm gonna move away
To Terlingua, Texas[15]

During a performance of his song at the Starlight Theatre, Trevor further underscored the difference between Austin and Terlingua when he paused between verses to notify an audience of tourists that "our closest traffic light is about an hour and a half away from here, and it's in Mexico."

Moving to the middle of nowhere does come with its own fair share of challenges, of course. There are only a handful of restaurants in town, and nightlife—other than music—is all but nonexistent. Many residents do not have access to the limited electric and water grids in South Brewster County, and those who do have grown accustomed to regular interruptions in service. Terlingua now has an ambulance and emergency paramedics, but it still has no other medical services, so many residents make a two-hour round-trip across the border into Ojinaga, Chihuahua, to visit a doctor or a dentist. Terlinguans must become self-sufficient in ways that city dwellers take for granted—by learning to cut their own hair, for example, or by building one's own home, as Trevor did. It is not uncommon for someone to move to the Terlingua area, persuaded by an avalanche of flowery testimony about the idyllic nature of rural living, only to realize after a few months or years that life in the remote desert can be filled with hardship.

"We call them broken dreams," said songwriter Jim Keaveny, in reference to the numerous abandoned homesteads that are scattered across Terlingua Ranch. "A lot of people think they want to live out here, so they buy up twenty acres and they build somethin' on it, and then they realize after a year or two of living here that it sucks. I mean, it doesn't *suck*, but it sucks to them. It's really windy and it gets extremely hot and extremely cold, and *blah-blah-blah-blah-blah*. And then they move off and leave their house just sittin' there." Jim made a wide sweeping gesture from where we stood on his front porch. "You don't realize it driving by on the highway, but a lot of these houses and trailers out here are empty."

While life in Terlingua is certainly not for everyone, those intrepid enough to stick around are often greeted with some big advantages over the cities they left. Among these is an extremely, almost absurdly low cost of living. "Moving to Terlingua is like getting a $30K-a-year raise," said Pat O'Bryan, which sounds like an exaggeration but is probably something of an understatement. This is partly due to cheap land: although property in the area immediately surrounding the Ghost Town now commands a hefty premium, in many of the outlying areas of South Brewster County, land can be found for as little as one hundred dollars an acre or even a quarter of that when purchased in larger tracts. Property taxes are also exceptionally low—often only twenty dollars per year for a typical five-acre plot. Moreover, the absence of building codes results in almost unlimited opportunities for creating low-cost alternatives to more traditional housing. For Trevor Reichman, this meant building a one-room, 250-square-foot adobe dome using freely harvested natural materials. Other residents live in straw bale houses, structures made of sandbags and old tires or beer cans and plaster, immobile school buses, trailers, teepees, tents, caves, pickup trucks, wooden gazebos enclosed in shade cloth—a myriad of housing solutions that would be downright illegal in most other parts of the United States.

Restrictions on off-grid living are also quite lax in South Brewster County, another feature that distinguishes it from much of the rest of the country. Whereas many states have laws on the books that limit rainwater catchment, Texas is home to some of the laxest rainwater laws in the nation—the state even offers tax breaks for people collecting rainwater on their property (all the more significant when considering that Texans pay no state income tax).[16] In Terlingua, where a public water utility is inaccessible for the majority of the population and where the sporadic water table can make drilling wells exorbitantly expensive (imagine drilling to 1,200 feet at a cost of $30 per foot, only to discover that the water is saline), the ability to collect an unlimited amount of rainwater for in-home use is a major reason that Terlingua is able to exist at all. Solar power is similarly unburdened by restrictions in South Brewster County, which, according to the US Department of Energy, happens to boast one of the best climates for solar energy in the nation.[17] When coupled with cheap land, this absence of regulation makes possible a low-cost lifestyle in Terlingua that would be financially impractical, if not illegal, in most other places in the United States. Almost anyone with a few thousand dollars can afford to buy a five-acre parcel of land, fashion a simple residence with a garden for food, set up systems for solar power, rainwater catchment, and a composting toilet, and then settle in to desert life with little in the way of monthly bills to pay.[18] I know a few Terlingua residents who live on less than $5,000 per year.

For someone accustomed to the high costs of the city, such a place can sound like a dream come true. Local songwriter Laird Considine recalled how this realization first hit him while he was living in Austin in the early 1990s, not long before he moved to Terlingua. "I was trying to find a job, and I was just doing crap," he told me. "I was really scrounging. Not getting any gigs, not getting any interviews, slowly going broke paying for an apartment. Then I got talking to Pam Ware [a longtime Terlingua resident who was visiting Austin], and I was like, 'You know Pam, I'm really tired of being here in the city. I'm thinking of moving to Terlingua. Do you have any advice?' And she says, 'Well, it's gonna take you a while to find a job, and you probably won't make much money, so I'd show up with a bit of a nest egg to see you through till you've figured out some way to make it work.' And I told her, 'I don't know what you mean by nest egg, but I've got about $8,000 saved up.' She just slapped her knee and laughed and said, 'Shit, you can *retire* in Terlingua!'"

The low cost of living is a great boon to all Terlingua residents, but it has proven especially advantageous for those pursuing music full-time. In this age of online music streaming services, when plummeting CD sales have forced professional musicians to rely more and more on live performances for their income, touring has become an increasingly important part of most musicians' annual calendars. Because of this, having an inexpensive home base that doesn't drain the bank account while you're living on the road is an enormous asset. Trevor Reichman spends up to half of each year touring, and this rigorous schedule is much easier to maintain now that he has no lease or mortgage payment. "Living here has really enabled me to do a lot of touring," he said. "Having a place that doesn't indebt me to it. I'm not paying rent or bills like in a city, where it wouldn't make sense to leave for too long a period and still pay for a place I'm not residing at that moment. It's nice to have a place where I can come and go as I please."

In addition to the substantially lower cost of living, most musicians moving to Terlingua are pleasantly surprised that gigs—particularly paying gigs—are much easier to procure. "In Austin, I couldn't find regular gigs," said Laird Considine. "But things worked out pretty miraculously when I moved here. On the day I arrived I stopped in at the Boatman's Bar & Grill, and a bunch of local musicians were having a weekly Tuesday night jam. It seemed they didn't have many bass players in town at that time. Well, I had all my gear with me, and next thing I know someone says, 'Hey, I got a gig at La Kiva this Friday. Would you be willing to play bass with me?' So suddenly I had my first paying gig and I'd only been in Terlingua for a few hours."

Blues guitarist Pat O'Bryan had much the same experience. "It's the demand curve in action," he observed. "I remember sending in my CD and my press kit for a free gig at a coffee shop in Austin, and after a few weeks, I hadn't heard anything, so I called up the person booking the venue, and she ripped me a new one for buggin' her. 'Do you realize how many CDs I've got on my desk right now?' Meanwhile, you've got people like Jimmie Vaughan and Charlie Sexton [both nationally renowned guitarists who got their starts in Austin], and they're playing for a hundred bucks a night just so they can play in their hometown. I can't compete with that. In Austin, there really are a hundred qualified, talented musicians for every gig. Here, there's not."

In his 1996 PhD dissertation on the Austin music scene, Jeffrey Farley revealed that guaranteed minimums were already becoming rare in Austin—only the most elite local acts received a guaranteed paycheck from the venue, while everyone else played solely for tips.[19] In Terlingua, by contrast, most gigs come with a guarantee, typically in the $50-$100 range for a solo musician performing a three-hour show. Audiences in Terlingua also generally tip well. In fact, a number of local and visiting musicians told me that Terlingua audiences are among the best tipping crowds they have ever played for, and it is not uncommon on any given night for tips to well exceed the check from the venue. While this admittedly amounts to a relatively modest source of income, in Terlingua it is still possible to live on "almost nothing but air," so each dollar earned goes much further in the desert than it would in the city. This holds true in my own experience. During the two years I spent in Terlingua, I was able to support myself modestly but entirely on music-generated income.

The internet has also changed the game considerably by making it much easier to pursue a music career remotely. One local resident uses his high-speed connection to do music production work from his home on Terlingua Ranch, while another rounds out her income as a full-time musician by teaching music classes online. I watched from the corner of the room as a singer-songwriter performed a paying gig from his computer on the online virtual world Second Life. Jim Keaveny, another ex-Austinite, used the crowd-funding sites Indiegogo and GoFundMe to raise money for his two most recent albums, both of which have found success in North America and Europe (his 2017 release *Put it Together* debuted at #15 on the EuroAmericana chart). For Trevor, Airbnb has made it possible for him to supplement his income by renting out the Dome while he is on the road, and his property's proximity to Big Bend National Park means that it is usually fully booked. Meanwhile, resources like indieonthemove.com, which allows musicians to independently book their own tours, have revolutionized the tedious process of coordinating and booking a tour, something that not long ago would have been prohibitively difficult while living in a place as remote as Terlingua. Personalized websites and social media pages have also made crafting an online presence easier than ever, while media-sharing platforms like YouTube make it possible for musicians to put their music in front of an audience without intermediaries like agents and record labels. YouTube in particular has proven to be a great equalizer, providing potential access to the commercial music industry for anyone with an internet connection, regardless of where they call home. This latter point was demonstrated in dramatic fashion in 2012, when Terlingua songwriter George Goss, with the help of several fellow Terlinguans, recorded and uploaded a music video for his song "Ain't No Honky Tonks in Jail" to YouTube. By the end of 2020, it had garnered almost 7 million views, ultimately landing Goss a publishing deal and a contract with country artist Johnny Bush to record the song.

Terlingua is not an ideal fit for every musician, of course. Like those "broken dreamers" who arrived in the desert only to feel stifled by the Big Bend's harsh conditions and limited resources, some musicians also find Terlingua's small size to be a source of frustration rather than opportunity. A few Terlingua musicians I spoke with admitted that they have played far fewer gigs after moving to Terlingua simply because they had already been A-list musicians in the cities they left, and Terlingua has far fewer venues in which to perform. Marti Whitmore, who holds two degrees in operatic vocal performance, expressed regret that she cannot perform recitals of classical music in Terlingua because there are no classical pianists in town to provide the accompaniment. Similarly, while Terlingua has proven to be a veritable haven for solo singer-songwriters, it can be a difficult environment for people wanting to form bands, as there is still a relatively small pool of players from which to draw. "It's tough," said Pat O'Bryan. "We have one drummer in this town, and he doesn't really want to play that much. Bass players, we've got a few, one who's got a full-time job that keeps him pretty busy. Sax players, we've got one. Lead guitar players, we have what, three? So if you're gonna put a band together in Terlingua, that's a pretty thin pool of players. But you can field as many poets with guitars as you want. We've got a *lot* of 'em."

It likely goes without saying that Terlingua will never be home to anything close to the number of professional musicians as Austin. For Trevor Reichman, however, that is precisely the point.

"If you were a tree sapling trying to grow in an over-crowded forest," he explained, "you wouldn't get the resources you need—the light, the water—because there's so much competition, so there is a very low chance of making it. In the desert, you have other obstacles, but there's more opportunity as far as having the resources to be able to build what it is that you do."

Aided by patience and a little creativity, Trevor and others like him have made the most of the opportunities provided by their desert home. Just as plants and animals evolve by cutting out niches for themselves in new environments, the handful of Terlingua musicians who earn their income from music have found their own niche within the professional music economy. By eschewing life in the traditional music capitals, these musicians have created their own paths to music careers. As life in urban areas becomes increasingly prohibitive, it appears they have done so at the perfect time.

However, as Terlingua's population grows and its music scene becomes better known outside the Big Bend, the future of the town's music economy has itself become a matter of uncertainty. A growing number of Austin musicians are now traveling to Terlingua to perform, and this increased competition for gigs, when coupled with the town's own steadily climbing population and cost of living, has led a number of local musicians to wonder how long this ideal musical climate will last. For some, these recent developments bear an uncanny resemblance, albeit on a much smaller scale, to the changes that began transforming the state capital several decades earlier.

"It's the Austin effect," said Trevor.

THE AUSTIN EFFECT

The holidays are easily the busiest time of the year in the Big Bend. With schools out and families on vacation, Terlingua and Big Bend National Park are crammed to the gills as people come from all over to enjoy the ample sunshine and moderate desert temperatures. The few weeks surrounding Christmas and New Year's are an especially busy time for music as well. The Starlight Theatre's annual New Year's Day tribute to Townes Van Zandt, an all-day celebration of the legendary Texas songwriter often hosted by Butch Hancock, is one of the highlights of the town's musical calendar each year, drawing dozens of performers from both Terlingua and afar. The annual Black-Eyed Pea Cook-off, a favorite event for many Terlinguans, often draws local musicians from decades past out of the woodwork to jam on the Porch. Venues, flush with revenue from crowds of vacationers, can afford to book full bands and A-list visiting acts in ways they cannot during slower times of the year. The Americana duo The Mastersons, perhaps best known as longtime members of Steve Earle's band The Dukes, make an annual appearance around this time, as does the Grammy-nominated Texas songwriter Jimmie Dale Gilmore.

The holidays in Terlingua spoiled me as a musician. I grew accustomed to having the kinds of memorable musical experiences that would have seemed remarkable only a few years before. I never thought I would have the opportunity to listen to a duo like The Mastersons in an intimate setting and then jam with them afterward around a kitchen table. Nor did I think I would ever get to perform some of my favorite Townes songs alongside songwriters who actually knew the man. Although I was always a bit relieved when the crowds began to thin out in mid-January and there was finally a little breathing room again on the Porch, in some ways the holidays became one of my favorite times to be a musician in Terlingua.

In January 2016, as one of the busiest two-week stretches of the year came to a close, Terlingua guitarist and blogger Pat O'Bryan reflected on the state of the local music scene. "There was some amazing music in Terlingua over the holidays," he wrote on terlinguamusic.com. "Butch and Rory Hancock, Jimmie Dale and Colin Gilmore, Gurf Morlix, The Mastersons, Bonnie Whitmore, Jacob Jaeger, Kristopher and Ann Wade, The Jitterbug Vipers, Will Taylor (Strings Attached), Chet O'Keefe . . . . And some locals also played—The Whitmores, The Fabulous Vortexans, Jim Keaveny and his band. From a consumer's point of view, it was a delicious smorgasbord of wonderful noises." Pat continued, noting how busy all the local venues were as residents and tourists came out to enjoy the music. "Our show at the Starlight Theatre was packed," he said, "and the Townes Van Zandt tribute at the Starlight was so packed that there was nowhere to stand or sit. The next night, there was an amazing show at La Kiva, and according to the sound guy, you couldn't have squeezed one more person in the room."

Despite the obvious success of these events, however, Pat also noticed something that led him to question the nature of what he was witnessing. "What, exactly, is Terlingua music?" he wondered. "Very few of the musicians who thrilled us over the holidays actually live in Terlingua. Strangely, the people on the stage and the vast majority of the people listening are from Austin, Dallas, San Antonio, Berlin, Amsterdam . . . not Terlingua."

Others noted this trend as well. "We are in the fourth distinct period of Terlingua's history," remarked river guide and fiddler Mark Lewis. "First, Terlingua was a mining town, and then it was a ghost town. In the 70s it became a river town. Now, Terlingua is a music town." Most Terlinguans would agree with this basic premise that their town is increasingly "on the map" as a place for music. Word of mouth, which continues to grow exponentially as more musicians travel to the Big Bend, has played a major role in this process, especially given the deep social and musical ties that still connect Terlingua with the state capital. Visiting musicians have noticed it, too. One Austin musician who had been visiting and performing in Terlingua for about five years told me that when she first starting gigging in Terlingua, hardly any of the musicians in Austin had heard of the town; today, she said, most of them know about it.

Anna Oakley, a Terlingua resident and musician, agreed. "When we first came out here from Austin and we told our friends where we were going, they didn't know where we were talking about. For years they didn't know what Terlingua is. But now? Now *everybody* knows what Terlingua is."

While word of mouth is likely the primary reason for this growing notoriety, internet exposure has also played a role in revealing Terlingua's music scene to the outside world. terlinguamusic.com, for one, has garnered a steady non-local readership since it was created in 2013; Pat estimates that, depending on the subject of the post, anywhere from 50 to more than 90 percent of the site's traffic now comes from outside Terlingua. During the 2014 South by Southwest festival, *Huffington Post* featured Terlingua in an article promoting "eight emerging cultural hotspots you should visit in Texas." The piece presented Terlingua as an alternative to the increasingly "corporate" and "circus"-like atmosphere of the Austin music scene. In other words, Terlingua was contrasted with Austin in precisely the same manner that Austin was contrasted with cities like New York and Nashville when the Texas capital was first gaining recognition as a destination for music.

Since I first arrived in Terlingua in 2013, a series of annual music festivals—Voices From Both Sides (founded in 2013), the Viva Terlingua Music Festival (held in 2014 and 2015), and Slim Fest (founded in 2016 in honor of the late Austin guitarist Slim Richey, who owned property in Terlingua)—have also increased outside exposure to the local music scene. The last two in particular have brought some of the biggest names in Austin music to perform in local venues. While none of these festivals were created with the intention of promoting Terlingua as a destination for music, each one has, in its own way, added to Terlingua's reputation as a music town. The founder of Viva Terlingua later expressed a tinge of regret about this, recognizing that the festival could have the unintended consequence of contributing to the same kind of musical saturation that motivated him and other Terlingua musicians to leave Austin.

When combined with the crisis currently besetting the Austin music scene, this increased exposure has resulted in more Austin musicians traveling to Terlingua for gigs. "I think the Austin explosion is a huge factor in what Terlingua is seeing," said one musician who grew up in Terlingua but who now calls Austin home. "It's so hard to get a good gig in Austin that bands are literally willing to drive to Terlingua for one."

Buckner Cooke, who booked music at the Starlight Theatre while I lived there, agreed. "When I got the job here, I suddenly became much more aware of how many people outside of Terlingua want to play here. On a normal day, I wake up and have a half-dozen emails from people wanting to perform at the Starlight. Some of it's local, but I would say 60 percent are from out of town. I really don't have to pull a lot of teeth to fill the schedule, and I'm having to turn a lot of people away."

For Austin musicians, Terlingua can be an attractive destination for a number of reasons. Both resident and nonresident musicians frequently comment that Terlingua audiences are among the most enthusiastic they have ever experienced. Trevor Reichman, who spends several months every year touring, said that Terlingua audiences are still "by far" the most enthusiastic he's ever witnessed. Many musicians also remark that bookers and venue owners in Terlingua are more gracious toward performers than their urban counterparts. "It always felt like the club owners in Austin thought they were doing you a favor by booking you," said Pat O'Bryan, who has played in venues all over the United States and Europe. "And then you get out here. You go play the Boathouse, and the people there are really *glad* to have that music to listen to. And Don's gonna feed you whatever you want to eat or drink. They're just delighted to make you feel comfortable. The only other place I've ever been like that was East Germany."

Of course, friendly venue owners and marginally better pay hardly seem like enough for most musicians to justify the almost one thousand-mile round-trip from Austin to the Big Bend. In order to offset their travel costs, many Austin musicians string together several gigs while in Terlingua by performing at all the local venues in a single weekend, a strategy that local booking managers have proven more than happy to accommodate. Visiting musicians also frequently pair gigs in Terlingua with gigs in nearby towns like Marfa and Alpine, thus creating a kind of mini-tour through the small but tourism-rich communities of the Big Bend.

The ever-increasing number of outside musicians coming to Terlingua to perform has made it much more difficult for local musicians to secure regular gigs. "In our first year here, we were performing every week," said Alex Whitmore, who moved to Terlingua full-time in 2010. "And then we got all the other newer musicians that have come into town that want to play, and there's just so many slots at the Boathouse and so many slots at the Starlight."

Singer-songwriter Laird Considine has had a similar experience. When he moved to Terlingua in 1992, there were only two regular paying music venues in town, yet music still made up a significant part of his annual income.

"I remember a spring break one year when I played twenty-three gigs in the month of March. That was the single biggest month of income I ever had. Plus, that was when I was livin' in a place that cost $50 a month. So with a $50 gig it was, 'Okay, covered October. Yeah, dude! I got six more $50 gigs comin' up, man. That covers me up until summer!' But now there's so much competition from the outside that I almost don't even bother trying."

The changes that Laird and others described were apparent even within my own comparatively brief time in the Big Bend. When I arrived in 2013, a number of Terlingua musicians had regular weekly residencies at local venues, and while it was not uncommon to hear out-of-towners performing on the weekends at the Starlight Theatre, local musicians were still playing the majority of the dates on the schedule. Today, it is unusual to see a local musician perform more than once or twice a month at the Starlight, while at the same time, the number of visiting musicians performing in Terlingua has increased dramatically. During a typical week today, fully half of the dates at the Starlight feature visiting musicians, the majority of them from Austin. Compounding the situation is the fact that venues are now often booked several months in advance, so that local musicians have to plan much further ahead and do a lot more "hustling" than they once did. For longtime Terlingua musicians, such changes constitute precisely the kind of "Austin effect" to which Trevor Reichman alluded.

All this increased competition for gigs is exacerbated by the fact that visiting musicians are often given the most lucrative gigs on the schedule, such as those occurring during holidays and weekends. While this makes sense from the visitors' perspective—after all, it would be difficult to justify a thousand-mile round-trip to perform for a half-empty room—it frequently leaves Terlingua musicians feeling like they are playing second fiddle to outside acts. "I've noticed that when the town starts getting busy, the locals will often get kind of punted to the side so that outsiders can come in and play," said Carol Whitney. "I get that people like variety, and it's good to be able to hear some different music in town. But just because it's busy and a bunch of Austinites want to come down and play, that doesn't mean you have to drop the locals in the best tip weeks. 'Cause frankly, a lot of the locals need the money."

Trevor Reichman agreed. "From an economic point of view," he said, "I find that it makes sense for venues to book locals as much as possible during the heavy tourism times. In those times, the venues are packed regardless, and the local musical acts, in which we are lucky to have such great quality, who know the protocol, and who have struggled during the off-season, can certainly benefit from the built-in audiences. The money that goes into the musicians' tip jars from tourists thus stays local and gets spent in our community starting the very next day. It makes more sense to book touring acts during slower times of the year to attract local residents who may be tired of hearing some of us local musicians by now. In those instances, the new music coming through becomes the attraction and increases turnout for the venues during slower times."

While the influx of visiting musicians has made Terlingua's gigging environment more competitive, it has arguably also led to a more entertaining musical atmosphere for local audiences. The people responsible for booking music in Terlingua's venues thus occupy a difficult position as they attempt to balance satisfying local musicians with gigs and satisfying local audiences with variety. "Let's face it," said Buckner Cooke, "if I never brought a single outside artist in, I could still keep the Starlight booked week after week with just local talent because we have that amount of talent. But because we live in a small town, we have only so many places to go eat, only so many places to go see live music.

The *real* juggling act is making sure that I throw enough business to the local musicians while also having enough variety that the local patrons want to keep coming back because there's always someone new to hear."

In addition to all this increased competition, some Terlingua musicians have told me that even when they do secure gigs, those performances often pay less than they once did—yet another feature of the "Austin effect" that Trevor described. "Musicians either attract less money on purpose or they attract less money unintentionally," said one Terlingua musician when I asked how the gigging atmosphere had changed during the past twenty years. Several people I spoke with were adamant that musicians who perform in commercial venues should be paid fair wages for their labor, a position they say has led them to play fewer gigs. "I've survived the entire spring without playing the Starlight," said one local musician who used to make more than $15,000 a year performing in Terlingua in the 1990s. "And I used to play it once a week. If the line of musicians or songwriters weren't there who play for free, and all the beer they can drink and a hamburger, then I would play more."

Laird Considine attributes the decreased number of paid local gigs specifically to the influx of Austin area musicians. "It's the Austinification of Terlingua," he said, unknowingly echoing Trevor's description. "There are so many more people and they're willing to play for way less. In Austin you pay to play, you compete, you're nonstop trying to get the gigs, it's very aggressive. Yes, the gigs in Terlingua pay less than they did twenty years ago when I moved here, but they still pay more than they do in Austin where they pay *nothin'*. So, I'm competing against all these young people for a $50 gig that used to pay 75 to 100. To me, it's not interesting to play a $50 gig. That's why a lot of the longtime local bands don't play around here anymore, they feel they're worth more than that. But the people who are comin' out here from Austin or wherever think that's great money.

Wow, you're gonna give me $50? Plus dinner and drinks and tips? Did I just move to paradise or what?"

Along with increased competition for performance opportunities and decreased pay for those performances, a third factor completes the trifecta that makes up the Austin effect as it exists in Terlingua: cost-of-living increases. A number of developments have coincided in recent years to make living in Terlingua more expensive. Not long ago, state property tax assessors visited South County for the first time in years, leading to fears that the area's uncommonly low property taxes are on the verge of rising. The cost of solar energy has also increased, due in part to a series of new tariffs placed on imported solar panels by the federal government.[20] Available for as little as one dollar per watt during my time in Terlingua, the price of solar panels has since tripled in the state of Texas, an increase that has been acutely felt by Terlingua's low-income, off-grid population.[21]

While the town has not experienced the same level of gentrification as Austin, many of the trends that have affected the state capital over the last several decades are beginning to be felt in Terlingua as well. Airbnb has become a major driver of the local economy, and the cost of land has risen sharply as both local and non-local investors continue to buy up plots for new vacation rentals. Meanwhile, several iconic local hangouts have undergone renovations and new injections of capital. Whereas t-shirts and bumper stickers that plead "Keep Austin Weird" can be seen all over the capital city, "Don't Marfa My Terlingua" stickers have become a regular sight in South Brewster County, in reference to another small town in the Big Bend that many locals believe has already "sold out."

Thanks to population growth and associated development, the ever-rising cost of living in and around the Ghost Town—the nucleus of Terlingua's musical life—has made it increasingly prohibitive for low-wage residents to live there. The price of undeveloped land in the five miles between the

Ghost Town and Study Butte has skyrocketed since the 1970s and can now be found advertised for more than $11,000 per acre. One Ghost Town resident told me that a two-acre plot near her home recently sold for $125,000, a fortune by Terlingua standards. As a result, just as Austin musicians have been increasingly displaced toward the outskirts of the city (or even farther), Terlingua musicians are increasingly marginalized to the periphery of South Brewster County, settling instead in outlying areas like Terlingua Ranch where land, for now, remains relatively inexpensive. "Even as comparatively low as the cost of living is in [the Ghost Town]," said Trevor, "I think it still somewhat prices out the creative class as far as ownership of land. It's getting to the point where someone in the creative class can't really afford to buy land in the Ghost Town, but anyone in the world can buy land in Terlingua Ranch if you're willing to put in a little work."

Because South Brewster County is so vast, this outward displacement significantly affects the extent to which residents living at the periphery of Terlingua can participate in the musical life of the Ghost Town. During my own time in Terlingua, I witnessed firsthand how Porch music lost some of its richness as several of its primary instigators moved farther from the center of town. Now, as Terlingua's population continues to grow, outlying areas are beginning to develop their own self-contained social scenes, and Trevor is hopeful that local music will follow the same path. "Being out here on the Ranch," he said, "I think it's gonna start happening maybe a little more. We've had some jams here in the Dome, and then you have Anna and Jim's house at times. This is starting to become its own little town in a way."

IT GOES WITHOUT SAYING that Terlingua will never come close to Austin in terms of population, congestion, or musical competition. Still, the similarities in their trajectories are hard to miss. For those Terlinguans who fled the state capital, only to find that many of the same trends that caused them to leave are now encroaching on their desert home, this process of change can feel a bit like a rising tide that is impossible to outrun. "If Austin was still the Austin I fell in love with in the 1970s, I'd still be in Austin," said Pat O'Bryan. "Terlingua . . . the last frontier . . . I guess Redford is next?" (Redford is an even smaller town, with a population of about one hundred people, about forty-five miles up the Rio Grande from Terlingua.)

Clearly, the issue of balancing local musicians with visiting musicians is not a simple one. While a few Terlingua musicians are wholeheartedly opposed to out-of-town performers—I heard one such person bitterly refer to musicians from Central Texas as the "Hill Country Mafia"—most local musicians have mixed feelings about the subject. On one hand, the opportunity to hear and interact with a wide variety of visiting performers, and to do so in a music scene as casual and intimate as Terlingua's, has long been a cherished part of life for many of the people who live there. To sit on the Porch in a tiny rural town and jam with someone like Alejandro Escovedo, Ramblin' Jack Elliott, Hal Ketchum, Butch Hancock, Steve Fromholz, Jimmie Dale Gilmore, or Joe King Carrasco—how many people have the privilege of experiencing that? On the other hand, most residents would prefer that their town and its music remain somewhat hidden, a "best-kept secret" in the wider world of Texas music. "I wish we could just sit here on the Porch and play music like we used to without anyone trying to put us on the map," said one local Porch musician during a break between songs, while several nearby tourists pointed cameras in his direction. "It's being found out," said another. "*Texas Monthly* magazine comes down here now; *Texas Highways* comes down all the time. And the more you have music festivals, the more you're just inviting the rest of the world here. If everybody would just shut up then maybe we could keep it hidden. But it's too late now. In terms of exposure, this place is already found out."

At the time of this writing, the pace of growth in major music cities around the country shows no sign of slowing. When I hear the testimonies of musicians who are struggling to make a living in places like Austin or Nashville or New York, I can't help but wonder how much longer such a state of affairs can possibly continue. If the cocktail of crises continues unabated, more and more musicians are almost certainly going to be forced to evacuate these increasingly crowded urban areas, whether by choice or necessity. Fortunately for them, there are now more resources than ever for those pursuing music careers outside the traditional music capitals, including technologies that allow musicians to record their music, upload it to fans, and book tours—all from the comfort of their living rooms. As the long-standing urban migration of musicians reverses its flow, and as performers are forced to develop new strategies for successful music careers, it is possible that the handful of Terlingua musicians who make their living from music will cease to be outliers, representing instead the vanguard of a new kind of professional musician. If so, they would join a growing army of remote workers in a plethora of other industries around the globe. While it is unlikely that the nation's music capitals will ever lose their relevance entirely, we may nevertheless be headed toward a future in which it no longer seems unusual to find songwriters like Trevor in small towns across the country.

Of course, leaving the city for a small town is not a cureall solution for musicians, and as Terlingua residents know firsthand, such rural migration can be a double-edged sword. Although population growth and the influx of musicians to Terlingua will likely result in a more varied music scene with more venues in which to play, the continuation of the current trend will eventually lead, as it has for Austin, to a tipping point. When will that tipping point occur? It depends on whom you ask.

A few years ago, Trevor traded his lumbering touring van for a Toyota Prius, and the increased fuel efficiency he gets as a result has helped to ensure that traveling for gigs remains lucrative. As the Austin effect becomes more pronounced in Terlingua, Trevor expects that he will have to rely even more on touring for his income. It is a change he says he is prepared to meet.

"I kind of think that this time frame from when I moved here till now was kind of an anomaly," said Trevor. "To be able to make a full-time livelihood playing music in a very small town that doesn't have a lot of wealth . . . I'm not expecting that to last."

CHAPTER 4

VOICES FROM BOTH SIDES

"I'VE SPENT A LOT of my life on this road," Collie Ryan mused. It was a sunny morning in February 2018, and Latin pop was on the radio as we cruised through the desert on Highway 170 between the Ghost Town and the Rio Grande. We were on our way to San Carlos, Terlingua's unofficial sister town, a small village nestled in the mountains of northeast Chihuahua about twelve miles south of the US-Mexico border.[1] The following morning, we and a few other Terlingua residents would be meeting with the mayor of San Carlos to discuss plans for the sixth annual Voices From Both Sides/Voces de Ambos Lados festival. Occurring each May on the banks of the Rio Grande between San Carlos and Terlingua, the festival features musicians from both towns as they take turns performing music back and forth across the river. As a longtime Big Bend resident and one of the only musicians to have lived in both Terlingua and San Carlos, Collie was the perfect person to lead the discussions.

Collie absentmindedly twirled one of the gray pigtail braids that flowed from underneath her cowboy hat, smiling from the passenger seat as she reflected on her long life in the stark country we now passed through. She arrived in the lower Big Bend in the late 1970s when the border in the region was still fluid, eventually building a house on the northern bank of the Rio Grande not far from the Lajitas river crossing that served as the thoroughfare between Ter-lingua and San Carlos. A low water spot with a hard rock riverbed, the Lajitas crossing has been in continuous use for centuries, one of the primary crossings in the hundreds of miles of steep-walled canyons that enclose the Rio Grande's course through the Big Bend. Eventually, two tiny villages sprung up on either side of the Rio, Lajitas on the US side and Paso Lajitas on the Mexican side. When Collie lived on the river, anyone could cross at any time, just as you might cross your own neighborhood creek on your way to work or the grocery store. No official checkpoint was necessary. The people living on either bank were a single community.

"Lajitas was my community, and Paso Lajitas was my community," Collie said. "Back then, it was a very multi-cultural area with the open border. You had the very rich mixing with the very poor, mixing with European tour-ists, mixing with boat people, mixing with Mexican people, and there was no class consciousness. It was just so peaceful. There was no sense of *I'm Mexican and you're white* or *I'm upper class and you're washing dishes*. We'd go in the bar in the afternoon and everybody'd be talking to everybody. It was just people."

At the turn of the twenty-first century, Paso Lajitas was a small but bustling town. "There was lots of kids, lots of fam-ilies," Collie recalled. "It was quite a busy little place. Two or three restaurants, a store. We used to have baseball games. Up above town there's a flat, and we had a team in Laja and a team in Paso, and everybody'd just drive the trucks across, laden with beer, and go up on top and play baseball. We'd have dances at the Trading Post. Had a band from San Carlos used to cross over and play for dances. And we'd have people come from the mountains, from way back in the outback, and people from San Carlos and all the ranchos and Terlin-gua. It was such an incredible mixture of people there at a dance. And a lot of people would just sit in their trucks, a lot of 'em would come dance, and there weren't no fights or nothin'. It was really nice. That was my community for twenty-odd years."

As we pulled into Lajitas and the Rio Grande came into view, Collie directed my gaze southward to where the buildings of Paso Lajitas were clearly visible a quarter mile or so across the river. Once home to as many as two hundred people, the town was now almost completely deserted. In the aftermath of the terrorist attacks on September 11, 2001, US Border Patrol officers descended upon Lajitas en masse. Arriving suddenly and without warning, they closed the historic crossing and arrested everyone they found on the wrong side of the river. Today, the crossing remains closed, and Paso Lajitas remains empty.

As I looked down at the muddy water of the crossing, it occurred to me how brief our journey from Terlingua to San Carlos would have been when the border here was still open. It is easy to forget now, but the Terlingua Ghost Town is nearer to San Carlos than it is to some of the outlying parts of the greater Terlingua area, and the people living on either side of this border are far closer to each other than they are to anyone outside the region. Once you've gotten a sense for how truly expansive and isolated the lower Big Bend is, it doesn't seem like such a stretch to imagine that local residents would consider people living just across the river to be their neighbors. I watched out the car window as we drove past the crossing, gazing down at the knee-deep water of the Rio Grande and the abandoned houses beyond as we continued westward on the highway.

Two-and-a-half hours later, we were finally in the State of Chihuahua and approaching San Carlos from the opposite direction when the Chisos Mountains again came into view. It was an arresting sight. We had traveled a long way to get here, driving upstream along the Rio Grande to cross through the nearest legal port of entry at Presidio-Ojinaga, only to turn around and head back downstream along the opposite bank. As anyone who has crossed an international border knows, such boundaries, with all their spectacle and infrastructure, can make you feel as if you are passing between two fundamentally different kinds of places. From our vantage point in northern Mexico, however, the Chisos looked almost exactly the same as they do from the Terlingua Porch. It is a strange sensation, feeling on one level that you are in a different world and on another that you've hardly left your front door. Everything I could see out the car window—the plant life, the shape of the mountains, the color and consistency of the earth—was perfectly familiar. Our car rounded a bend and startled a covey of scaled quail that rocketed off into the distance. I could have been watching them from my own trailer window. I had traveled across plenty of international boundaries in my lifetime, but most of them I had crossed by plane. This felt categorically different. Now that I was experiencing it from ground level, the very idea of borders seemed suddenly artificial. I thought about the residents of Terlingua and San Carlos, on whom this arbitrary line had only recently been imposed. What did "border" mean for them?

Big Bend photographer Jim Bones once remarked that "rivers are unifiers, not dividers." Nowhere is this truer than in the desert. In places where life-giving water is so precious and scarce, perennial water sources almost inevitably become gathering places and centers of civilization. Throughout most of Big Bend history, the Rio Grande has been such a place. For millennia, humans have been making their homes indiscriminately on both banks, crossing from one side to the other with no more concern than New Yorkers crossing the Hudson or DC residents crossing the Potomac. In the twenty-first century, however, politics has drawn a line through an area where previously none existed, destroying a way of life that predates either of the two countries in question. Terlinguans and their neighbors across the river would like to see a return to some semblance of normal in their tucked-away corner of the borderlands. Today, a handful of local musicians are trying to make that dream a reality.

ON THE RIO

Most of us who don't spend our lives near international boundaries are conditioned to think of borders as dividing lines—tangible margins where one kind of place ends and another begins. The border in the Big Bend, however, has historically been extremely fluid. Although there have never been any crossings of national consequence in the region (the population density is much too low), as recently as 2002, residents on both sides of the Rio Grande crossed back and forth daily, without paperwork, at a series of unofficial crossings connecting the small communities interspersed along the river. This arrangement was borne out of practical necessity. Because these towns are isolated in a vast sea of otherwise uninhabited desert, they have long relied on each other for the most basic of necessities. People living in Lajitas and Terlingua would cross the river to buy produce or eat in a restaurant, while people living in San Carlos and Paso Lajitas would cross for work, for school, to check their mail, or to buy goods like gasoline that were more difficult to procure south of the river.

Thanks to the ease of crossing, residents on both sides of the Rio became socially and economically intertwined. "It was one town with a river running through it," said Charlotte Teer. Collie Ryan agreed. "It was one community. We'd go down to the Lajitas Trading Post and play pool and drink with the Mexican people and then go across the river. You took the boat across and went shopping or you had lunch over there. It was just a really unique experience to live that way. It was a good community, a good feeling."

Long before the Terlingua Ghost Town was resurrected, Lajitas was the social and economic hub for an enormous swath of remote desert on both sides of the Rio Grande. "The Lajitas Trading Post was the center of the universe for a huge expanse of rural Mexico and the United States," said Bill Ivey, who grew up in South Brewster County and who eventually took over ownership of the Trading Post from his father, Rex. "We had dances at the Trading Post that were just legendary. It was not uncommon to have dances that lasted all night, and there were many times I'd go out at nine o'clock in the morning and pull the plug and say, 'That's enough, go home! We gotta clean up now!' We had incredible memories at some of those dances. It was the Old West. You can imagine a saloon scene with people dancing around and shooting guns through the ceiling. You put that on the border and that is what was literally happening. It would be real corny to try and write it the way it actually happened."

For decades, the northern Chihuahuan city of Ojinaga, located on the river about sixty-five miles upstream from Terlingua, has been a major hub for música norteña, an accordion-driven style of dance music popular in the borderlands. Mexican bands touring in the United States would often cross the river at Lajitas when they did not have the documentation necessary to pass through one of the major border crossings. "Lajitas was a real popular crossing for that area of Mexico at that time," said Ivey, "and many of the bands that were coming across into the United States to play would cross there because somebody in the band didn't have their papers. And 99 percent of the time they would stop and ask me if they could play on the porch and pass the hat. So I'd give them a tank of gas and let them pass the hat and we'd have an act for Thursday night. Looking back, one of those bands came to be Conjunto Primavera. It'd probably cost $20,000 or $30,000 to get them to play now. And here they were, playing in Lajitas."

Like many of the children who grew up in the area, Kelly Sufficool was raised on both sides of the Rio Grande. "Growing up, it never felt like I was entering another country," she recalled. "Both cultures were so intertwined in Terlingua, Lajitas, and Paso Lajitas that it never felt like you were entering another country going over to Paso. It was just the other end of town that you had to cross the river to get to. There was really no Border Patrol presence at that time, none of the scrutiny that you see today. It was just an informal crossing. In high school, you made plans to go to friends' birthday parties on both sides, without even *thinking* about the fact that you were going to Mexico. It was just one community that happened to have this little bitty strip of brown water that ran through it for most of the year."

Although Kelly was an American citizen and possessed no official papers granting her the legal right to live in Mexico, she spent most of her childhood living on the south side of the river in Paso Lajitas. Each morning, she and her classmates would catch a boat ride across the Rio Grande to attend school in Terlingua. When Kelly was in high school, as much as a third of the enrollment at the Terlingua school came from students who lived on the opposite bank. "It would be pitch black in Paso when we got up in the morning," she recalled. "And we'd walk down to the boat crossing by flashlight and meet the rest of the kids from Paso, and they'd row us across the river. On top of the hill on the US side was an old van that doubled as a school bus, and Howard Chandler Sr. drove the van with all of us kids to the school. I don't ever remember the Border Patrol trying to stop that boat. There was never any worry."

Paso Lajitas was even more isolated from its nearest neighbors in Northern Chihuahua than Terlingua is on the Texas side. In addition to sending their children across the river to attend school, many Paso Lajitas residents relied on the unofficial crossing for work. Most of the people who took the rowboat on a daily basis had jobs in Lajitas, while those who remained in Paso generated income from the daily stream of tourist traffic that came across the river. "It used to be that people would come here, and if they only had a day, there are just a few gems that they *had* to do," said Cynta de Narvaez, who has worked in the tourist industry in various capacities since moving to Terlingua in the mid-1990s. "Back then, the gem was go to Paso Lajitas and have breakfast, and watch the ostriches, and maybe pick up some eggs and come home. That was *awesome*. It tied the two sides together so nicely."

Everyone was aware, of course, that daily life in the lower Big Bend existed in a kind of legal gray area. Whenever a Border Patrol vehicle was spotted, word spread around town, and everyone made sure they returned to the "correct" side of the river. "We always had a system in place," Kelly recalled. "If you were hanging out in Terlingua, and you saw the Border Patrol go past, you'd call your buddy in Lajitas and say, 'Hey, there's two vehicles headed your way, give everybody a heads up.' And everybody would jump on their horses or in their trucks and go right back across the river. And the Border Patrol would come around to the Trading Post, and the pool table would be deserted—before there might've been a party goin' on, you know—and everybody would be gone. And Border Patrol would come through and make a circle, go in and get some potato chips and maybe some fuel, and then they'd leave. And then twenty minutes later, the party would resume. Whoever was playing the game of pool would continue their game, and everybody would go back to normal."

That normal way of life that had existed in the lower Big Bend for decades came to a screeching halt on the morning of May 10, 2002. It was an otherwise quiet Friday, and the early summer heat was just beginning to take hold when Border Patrol agents drove down to South Brewster County as they had done on countless occasions. This time, however, something was different. People had long been accustomed to seeing officers in the area, but it was almost always only a few vehicles or agents at a time, and their presence was rarely more than a formality. On this day, however, Border Patrol agents arrived suddenly and unexpectedly en masse, with a fleet of vehicles, numerous officers on the ground, and even a helicopter. "We immediately knew something was happening," recalled Kelly. "People were going, 'Oh my gosh, there's a whole *lot* of vehicles. Is there a raid? What's going on?' Nobody knew. I know I had *never* seen that amount of law enforcement show up at one time. Ever."

The raid was code-named "Operation Green River Tours," and Border Patrol officials described it as an ordinary patrol. "It is very routine for us whenever [we] are conducting an operation to use helicopters and that number of agents," Marfa Border Patrol spokesman Pablo Caballero told a reporter after the raid. "Maybe for (Lajitas residents) it's not routine, because they're not used to it, but it's going to be routine."[2]

Local residents were stunned. "It was such a shock," said Kelly. "I remember when the helicopters descended upon us. No one had ever seen helicopters like that except in the movies. We'd never seen that volume of Border Patrol, law enforcement, the unmarked law enforcement and unmarked vehicles. It was as if somebody had decided to raid the whole area at once."

Collie Ryan remembers that day vividly as well. "They came down," she recalled. "And there was a sixteen-year-old kid who rowed this old leaky rowboat that we used to cross the river. And they brought a big semi truck down, and they arrested the sixteen-year-old boy and took him away. And they took the boat and put it in the truck and reported it as an *aquatic invasion vehicle*. It was payday that day, so everybody was there. And they stormed in and just swept up people and threw them in the buses. Women, old women, kids, children . . . it was awful. They had a helicopter running up and down the river, it was just ridiculous. It changed the world here. It just changed everything."

Operation Green River Tours was part of a much larger crackdown that occurred along the entire US-Mexico border following the September 11 attacks of the previous year.

4h

Local residents were quick to point out that none of the terrorists responsible for those attacks were Mexican, nor had
any of them crossed into the United States via its southern
border. "I understand the 9/11 reaction," said Kelly, "because
I was watching on live TV as the second plane hit the second
tower. Those shockwaves were felt clear to the border, clear
to the river. But none of us could understand why they shut
down the border *here*. The 9/11 terrorists certainly didn't
come through Mexico. But after 9/11 it just didn't matter. It
was completely closed. There was no gray area, no informal
crossing anymore at all. All of a sudden, there was an invisible hard line between Lajitas and Paso Lajitas."

The Border Patrol arrested twenty-one people during the
unannounced raid in May 2002. The teenager who had been
manning the rowboat that day, a Mexican citizen and a student at Terlingua High School, was arrested on suspicion of
illegally transporting people across the border and was kept
in custody for nearly two months. One person who was present recalled that fifty Terlingua residents attended the teenager's arraignment eighty miles north in Alpine.

For the millions of people living along the two thousand-
mile-long US-Mexico border, the increased restrictions that
followed 9/11 were surely an inconvenience. For Big Bend
residents, however, the closure was truly devastating. The
abrupt closing of all the region's unofficial crossings left
the Big Bend with a single legal crossing in a section of the
border more than five hundred miles long—nearly a quarter
of the US-Mexico border's total length. Under the new restrictions, people wishing to pass from Lajitas to Paso Lajitas,
hardly more than a stone's throw from each other, now had
to travel fifty miles to the nearest port of entry at Presidio,
Texas, cross the border into Ojinaga, Chihuahua, then travel
for hours on rough dirt roads in order to reach Paso Lajitas
from the south. A quick jaunt of a few seconds had overnight become a full day's journey. "It was as if one day, all of
the sudden there was an invisible wall now," recalled Kelly.

"It went from *we're one community* to *you can't see your neighbors or your friends or your family*, unless you make an all-day trek. It turned into an ordeal, especially if, like a lot of us, you didn't have a good working vehicle."

For the people living in Paso Lajitas and San Carlos, many of whom relied on the crossing for their livelihoods, life on the river quickly became impossible. Chevo Garcia has lived his entire life in San Carlos. Before the closure, Chevo—an accordionist and saxophonist—would cross the river at Lajitas with his band to play gigs in Terlingua. "We used to come over with a truck and everything," he told me. "Before, there was a lot of crossing for business and work. We could go across to the store, and we'd just buy whatever we needed. And now you can't cross. It makes it very difficult, and poorer, because before when it was open there was lots of tourism that came to San Carlos. People would cross here and it was never a problem."

Because the closure of the Lajitas crossing prevented both workers and tourists from crossing the river, families in Paso Lajitas were forced to move farther into the interior of Chihuahua in order to make a living. "Paso went from a thriving town to a ghost town in a matter of months," said Kelly. "And I grew up on both sides, so that was really hard to watch." Kelly recalls that most of the students who rode with her every morning on the rowboat were the first in their families to receive high school diplomas. As it happens, hers was the final class at Terlingua High School to graduate before the border was closed. At twenty-four students, it remains the largest graduating class in school history.

Families whose members lived on both sides of the river felt the closure of the Lajitas crossing most acutely of all. Many of these families had split citizenship—some members were US citizens, others were not. When the border was closed, those who could legally remain in the United States were faced with an impossible choice: stay in the United States and enjoy the benefits therein—such as higher wages for parents and better educational opportunities for children—or forego those benefits and return to Mexico with the rest of the family. Those who were undocumented residents of the United States risked being arrested and deported if they attempted to cross the river to see family members. For many families, the result of this choice was heartbreaking: with no work and no possibility of crossing the river to see family on the other side, there was no longer any reason to remain in the Big Bend. "It tore families apart instantly," said Kelly. "Those who had papers and citizenship stayed in Texas to try to make a better living. And the ones who didn't, not only could they not stay near their family in Lajitas, just to survive they had to go farther into Mexico where there was work. It was really hard. You would have a family of four or five, and the two older kids would've been born in Mexico, and the two younger kids would've been born in Texas. So the two older kids had to stay with one parent in Mexico and the two younger kids had to go with the other parent. It was a really rough time for a lot of families."

It has been two decades since the Lajitas crossing was shut down. At the time of this writing, it remains closed to all traffic. Local residents have long hoped that the crossing might someday be reopened and the binational community in the Big Bend restored, but no official plans to that effect have ever been proposed.

The first ray of hope in an otherwise dark decade finally came in spring 2013. Following a long battle by area residents and local government officials in both countries, one of the Big Bend's unofficial crossings reopened for the first time since 2002, reconnecting Big Bend National Park with the tiny town of Boquillas del Carmen, Coahuila. The crossing, which is located about fifty miles to the southeast of Terlingua, has long offered park visitors the opportunity to cross the river into Boquillas, whose economy is entirely reliant on tourism. The newly reopened crossing is no longer informal. There is a multi-million dollar Border Patrol facility there now, and crossings are strictly limited, with restricted hours and traffic that goes almost entirely one way. Still, the renewed flow of tourists into Boquillas has breathed new life into a town that, like Paso Lajitas, had been all but deserted since the border was closed.

The new Boquillas crossing opened just as I was beginning my research in Terlingua, and one of the first events I participated in after arriving in the Big Bend was a small festival in Boquillas celebrating the reopening. The event was attended mostly by area residents, including a number of Terlingua musicians who performed as part of the day's festivities. Everyone seemed ecstatic by the resurrected crossing, sure that the town across the river would be revitalized by the new influx of tourism. As joyous as the occasion was, however, it also served to highlight the fact that the Lajitas crossing remained closed, and that without a similar plan for reopening, the devastating effects of the closure on the intertwined communities of Paso Lajitas and South Brewster County were sure to continue.

On the eleventh anniversary of the closure, one Terlingua musician devised a plan to do something about it.

VOICES FROM BOTH SIDES

Jeff Haislip is as effortlessly gregarious a figure as you will find in Terlingua. Previously a car salesman in Austin, he moved to the Big Bend in 2010, trading a lucrative career in the capital city for a slice of small-town desert life. In physical appearance, Jeff fits the Terlingua mold, sunbaked and eminently casual. He has bright blue eyes and a full beard, his curly graying hair tucked neatly beneath a sweat-stained straw cowboy hat. His pearl-snap plaid shirt is rolled up at the sleeves and left open several buttons down from the collar revealing a thick mass of chest hair. He wears cowboy boots with cargo shorts—a major fashion faux pas in urban Texas—and he doesn't bother removing his boots before wading, big-grinned and giddy, into the muddy waters of the Rio Grande.

Although Jeff is relatively new to Terlingua as a full-time resident, he has been a regular visitor to the area for decades. He remembers when the border in the Big Bend was fluid, something that to him seemed perfectly normal for the region. "I've been going over to Mexico since the 80s," he told me, "and it used to be that you could just go back and forth all you wanted to. I mean, you're going to Mexico to have lunch and a beer. You're not going over to do anything heinous. It's just a change of scenery. I grew up in Kansas City, and guess what, I was born on one side of the Missouri River, but I grew up on *both* sides of the river. So to me this isn't a big stretch."

Like the overwhelming majority of Terlingua residents regardless of political persuasion, Jeff is vehemently opposed to the border closure in the Big Bend. He believes it is easy for government officials and people living in the interior of the country to advocate for tighter border restrictions while failing to understand how such restrictions affect the lives of border residents, especially those in the remote Big Bend region where crossing the river has historically been a nonissue. "They just don't understand what situation we're in right here," Jeff said. "It's real easy for the government to look out here and say, 'You know, it's only a couple hundred miles out of the way to cross somewhere else.' I mean, come *on!*" He threw up his hands indignantly. "But that's what they do. I'm not saying that's what they're *trying* to do, but that's what they do. They divide. They separate. And that doesn't promote anything."

Jeff recounted a pair of personal experiences that convinced him that some kind of action was in order. The first occurred not long after he moved to Terlingua. "I was tending bar down at Lajitas," he said. "These tourists came in from Vermont, a couple of high-up administrators in the Vermont public education system. And they're asking about the area and I'm answering their questions, and then naturally the conversation goes to Mexico. And one of them said, 'Hey Jeff, I know you Texans hate Mexicans . . . .' And I was like, '*What?*' That was what they thought. Their perception is that we're all against each other. But that's not the truth right here." The second event occurred not long before I met Jeff when he crossed the border to visit San Carlos. "I asked some people when I was over there how the border closing affected them," he recalled. "And one guy says, 'Imagine if you were in South Korea, and you were looking north at North Korea, and you were wondering, *how are we going to get these guys to open up this border?*' It about floored me when he said that because as Americans, we always think we're justified in everything we do. That got me thinking."

Convinced that something needed to be done, Jeff started brainstorming. A singer-songwriter, he pondered the resources that small and largely poor Terlingua might have at its disposal, and before long he was struck with a simple idea: *they might be able to prevent us from crossing the river, but they can't prevent our music from crossing.* Out of this kernel of inspiration, the Voices From Both Sides festival was born. With considerable assistance from residents of both Terlingua and San Carlos, Jeff worked out the nuts and bolts of the event in a matter of months, even securing official permission from the US Border Patrol to ensure that no one would be arrested for wading into the river.

The first annual Voices From Both Sides/Voces de Ambos Lados festival occurred on the banks of the Lajitas crossing on May 11, 2013, almost eleven years to the day after the crossing was closed. The inaugural event was a simple affair. Residents set up amplification systems and rudimentary stages on either bank, and local musicians from Terlingua and San Carlos took turns playing back and forth across the Rio Grande while others barbecued, threw Frisbees, and danced in the river. The San Carlos-based Conjunto La Furia Norteña, the family band of the aforementioned accordionist and saxophonist Chevo Garcia, provided the music on the Paso bank. La Furia had brought the far superior sound

Jeff Haislip (in the straw cowboy hat) performs with Terlingua musicians at the Voices From Both Sides festival, 2017.

system, and their infectious blend of cumbia and norteño had attendees dancing all day long as they traded songs with a few dozen Terlingua musicians across the river. When their time came to play, Los Pinche Gringos—the only Terlingua-based band that plays the styles of Mexican music popular in the borderlands—carried their instruments across the river to perform on the opposite bank. Early in the proceedings, Ramón García Zapata, then the mayor of San Carlos, and Bill Ivey, the longtime owner of the Lajitas Trading Post, current owner of the Starlight Theatre, and the closest person Terlingua has to a mayor, waded into the middle of the river to ceremoniously hug and shake hands. Later that afternoon, with Border Patrol officers watching from a hill overlooking the river, residents of both countries joined hands to form a symbolic bridge across the Rio Grande.

Kelly Sufficool recalls how meaningful the inaugural Voices From Both Sides event was for the people who had once called both sides of the river home. "It's funny," she said. "The very first year we did this, everybody was kind of hesitant. Everybody on both sides had kind of gone towards the middle of the river, but the Border Patrol was parked on the hill. *Can we go all the way across and hug these people we haven't seen? Or are they gonna descend upon us again?* And then, I don't know who broke the ice, but once we started going back and forth across, *then* it felt like a party. It felt like it used to, like a homecoming. I did so much hugging and crying that first year. It was very emotional. My friends got to see family members they hadn't seen in years. I got to see a classmate I hadn't seen since I graduated who was there with her young daughter. I got to see her parents who used to own the store in Paso. I got to see a lot of the people I had graduated with. So for me, it was kind of a mini class reunion in a sense. Getting to see people I hadn't seen in that area, in that town, for *years*, it was . . . like I said, it was lots of hugging and crying."

Other than a 2020 cancellation due to COVID-19, the Voices From Both Sides festival has been held every year since 2013. Attendance at the event has steadily grown— I estimate that more than five hundred people attended in 2018, the last year I was present. A large part of this growth is due to the fact that families who were separated by the closure in 2002 are now coming from much farther afield. I spoke with people at the 2018 festival who had come from as far away as Midland-Odessa (250 miles to the north) and Chihuahua City (200 miles to the southwest) to see family members who lived across the border.

The festival has also attracted interest from national press, including write-ups in the *New York Times*, the *Nation*, and *Al Jazeera*. This exposure has brought outside attendees who have no personal connection to the area. Despite this, Voices remains a staunchly locals-oriented event. It is not a "festi-val" in the same sense as the commercial music festivals that take place in the summertime throughout the United

States. Attendance at Voices is completely free and requires no ticket for entrance. Local residents on both sides of the river donate their time and money each year to provide the food, stages, shade structures, sound systems, and other infrastructure that is required in order for the event to take place. Musicians sign up to perform just as they would at an open mic in Terlingua. One organizer described the event— accurately, I think—as a "family picnic."

Most Terlingua residents believe that Voices From Both Sides has been a resounding success and a much-welcomed response to current border policy in the region. "This party we have on the border is such a wonderful thing," said Collie Ryan. "It's rare that two sides of a border should celebrate their community in the world. Maybe we're the only one, or at least the only one that's getting any press. 'Cause most of the border thing is just *peck peck peck peck*, you know, like two roosters facing off. But for some reason, this event has Velcroed into people heavy. It touches a chord in people. And not just the people who remember the days when the crossing was open, but *lots* of people."

Terlingua songwriters have been particularly enthusiastic about Voices and the transnational sense of community that inspires it, and they have written a whole catalogue of original songs that deal specifically with the border, its closure, and local responses to the ongoing crisis. In "Getting Fatter," Laird Considine references the border closure, portraying it as one of the biggest changes in Terlingua's history:

> I remember I was working in Lajitas that day
> When the Twin Towers burned to the ground
> And I remember that black Friday
> When our border got shut down
> And our lives here in the Big Bend
> They got more complicated
> And the man who was our President then
> Was a man I sure hated[3]

Collie Ryan performs at the Voices From Both Sides festival, 2014.

The US Border Patrol ramped up their presence in the Big Bend dramatically in the months and years following 9/11, much to the frustration of many Terlingua residents. In her song "Little Green Men," which references the green Border Patrol uniforms, Bryn Moore brilliantly reverses the concept of "alien," using the term to refer, not to undocumented immigrants, but rather to the Border Patrol agents themselves—the real group that most Terlinguans believe don't belong in the Big Bend:

Pretty soon we'll all be overrun
An invasion of little green men
Our president says our borders are porous
He wants to fix that and
He's sending more little green men down here
To be at his beck and call
For those of us living down here on the border
We'll have no more worries at all

For those of us living down here on the border
We'll have no more worries at all[4]

Some of these songs are written from the perspective of residents of the small towns south of the river for whom the closure has been especially challenging. In "Guadalupe," Alex Whitmore imagines a woman for whom the closure has meant a lost job and a fractured family:

In days not very long ago
In a border town in Mexico
Life was good
A short ride in a flat boat
Meant a job and a payday
That she understood
But now the big man on the other side
Has stopped the boats and killed the pride
Of self-support
And a lover from a land so close
She could throw a stone to has left
To fight a war

Guadalupe
The desert flowers reflecting in those dark eyes
Guadalupe
Will you ever see the man of your desire?
In this ever-changing world
Will you find your way to happiness and good times?
Guadalupe
In your loving arms a baby cries

Now a border town in Mexico
Without a crossing it can't go
On living
And a woman with a little girl
Is left to see a world
That's unforgiving

And lately she just wants to cry
As the rafters float the river
She can wade across
But it all seems so unfair
It makes it just too hard to bear
The loss[5]

Other songs, such as Trevor Reichman's "Olé Song," are written from the perspective of people on the Texas side of the border who desire to know their neighbors living on the opposite bank:

I see you in your boat across the river
You're in my view, I see your shadow shiver
I see your silhouette shimmer against the flicker of your
    fire

I don't know you but I want to
We're a stone's throw away, but it might as well be two . . .
    million
Let's meet in the middle of the mire[6]

Finally, a number of songs in the last five years have been written about Voices From Both Sides itself, including Jeff Haislip's "Fiesta Protesta," which is loosely written in the polka-based style that typifies much norteño and Tejano music:

On the border we like to have fun
But we don't want to get arrested
Bring your guitar and meet me down the Río
Let's have a fiesta protesta [protest party]

Fiesta protesta
Comida y cerveza [food and beer]
Para bailar en el río [in order to dance in the river]
Amigos necesito [I need friends]

A peaceful party and a protest
How we've been torn apart
Fiesta protesta
Libere la Frontera [free the border][7]

As welcome as Voices From Both Sides has been for Terlingua residents, the annual event has been especially meaningful for people living on the south side of the river, many of whom have felt the effects of the border closure much more acutely. "It means a great deal, this day," said Chevo Garcia, who performs at Voices every year with Conjunto La Furia Norteña. "It gives us hope that the river will never be totally closed like it was before. It's sad, because you can't cross. Nobody can cross. But every year, we get to meet together and we get to spend a little time together. It's a celebration that really comes with God. We'll do it as long as we can do it, and when they stop it, we'll stop. But we want it to keep going year after year with even more people."

The mayor of San Carlos, María de Jesús Villanueva Villa, described how she felt the first time she attended Voices From Both Sides in 2017. "It was very beautiful, and very sincere," she said. "I'd never been to an event, and I repeat, I'd *never* been to any event like this ever. And it filled me with emotion. It's an event of finding ourselves and getting with our families and our relatives and our neighbors. It's a time of getting together and continuing the combination and the union that we have between our two towns. One thing that touched me was that we were able to serve food to each other from either side of the water that's not supposed to be crossed. That's another detail that's very beautiful and very important. We're lucky to be in a moment where we fear this won't be a problem. Let's hope there's not something that changes, some factor that will keep this from happening again." Villa also echoed other participants in saying that the most important part of the festival was the opportunity it provides for families to be reunited. "For me,"

Meeting in the river at the Voices From Both Sides festival, 2018.

she said, "the most important thing was that the families from the United States and from here came and found each other. This event is the type of thing to help people so they can find themselves with their families, even after years of not seeing each other. Now they know that there's an event every year where they can come see each other and be together and share together, live together and be close to each other. It's an event full of emotion, full of happiness."

However, Villa also recognizes the broader symbolic importance that Voices holds in our current political era. "These events don't have a price," she said. "And thank God for it. Because the state we're in right now is forgotten in that moment. Everybody forgets about their problems, everybody forgets about the differences between our two countries. The event on the river is the only one like it in the world. It is something that is needed on our Earth, it is something that is needed in all different countries. And we will continue while we can."

I asked Jeff Haislip what he hopes Voices From Both Sides will achieve moving forward. His greatest wish is that the festival might begin a conversation that will eventually lead to the reopening of the Lajitas crossing, so that a once bi-national community might once again flourish. While that still seems a long way off, Jeff hopes that in the more immediate future Voices might help to change how people in the United States view their southern border, the people who live there, and even borderlands more broadly. "You know, there's borders all over the place," he mused. "And look at all the division that has happened around the world when these borders are put up. I don't have any answers. I have more questions than answers. But if we can have a little bit more awareness in the future, then we might be able to make better decisions."

The Voices From Both Sides festival has only become more relevant in recent years. In June 2015, Donald Trump announced his candidacy for president with a plan to build a wall along the US-Mexico border. During his campaign, and continuing after his election, the Trump administration's language and policies concerning Mexico and immigration have threatened to usher in a new era of social and cultural division, a trend that has had an outsize influence on people living in the borderlands where the two countries meet. Terlingua and its neighboring towns have already felt the impact of one round of restrictions—even decades after the closure in 2002, locals are still dealing with its effects. Now, with the US-Mexico border again a regular part of the national political conversation, the Voices festival suddenly seems more significant than ever.

Many longtime residents of Terlingua—those who were around before the border was closed—believe that the fluid nature of the international boundary in the Big Bend made the people who lived there safer. One resident who provided humanitarian aid across the river after the closure pointed out that many residents of small towns in rural northern

Mexico saw their employment opportunities evaporate after the 2002 raid. Consequently, it became much easier for drug cartels to recruit in the area. (Significantly, US Border Patrol records show that the Big Bend sector sees the least amount of illegal activity of any part of the US-Mexico border by a large margin, despite being easily the largest sector by mileage.[8]) Chris Muller, another longtime resident, said that the bonds of community that extended across the river also helped make people safer. "What the people in Washington don't understand is that when we were neighbors," she said in 2015, "we had communication, we looked out for each other, we were friends. And then you put up this imaginary wall, and now he [Trump] wants to build a real wall. But that isolates people more than it helps them, I think. I mean, poor Trump lives in Washington and he has all these bad feelings, whereas if you live along the border, you don't have these bad feelings. You look over there and you go, 'God, it looks just like Texas.' Those people, they're humans, and, just like us, they're tryin' to get by in this godforsaken part of the world."

Voices From Both Sides originally had nothing to do with Trump. After all, the festival was created in 2013, two years prior to Trump's candidacy, as a means of protesting the closure of the Lajitas crossing more than a decade earlier. However, given the political developments in the years since, Voices has been reimagined by some participants, not only as a protest of the original 2002 closure, but also as an explicit protest of Trumpian politics, his proposed wall, and the divisive discourse he has championed. "I just think we need to be louder and louder about the issue," said Bryn Moore in 2018, when I asked her about the increased relevance of Voices during and after the Trump era. "We need to push back against the way things are going."

Terlingua resident Sha Reed Gavin also believes that the festival has received more traction in recent years due to the current political division in the United States. "I really think that the majority of people still come to Voices because they want to make that message clear that this crossing needs to be open," she said during the festival in 2018, "but I *absolutely* think it's also a protest of the wall. This is the most people I've ever seen here. This is almost twice as many as two years ago. And I think there's a lot of people here who went out of their way to make that statement. I've heard [people] say that they hope it gets back to Washington that this many people are coming out, celebrating, hoping that the border will be reopened as opposed to a wall being put up."

Once again, Terlingua songwriters have used music to voice their opposition to a border wall in the Big Bend. Trevor Reichman's "Walls Divide" speaks to the issue head-on:

Walls divide people into sides
It hasn't worked yet
If you want to connect
Build a bridge instead
Walls divide neighbors from their allies
And that's not safe
If you want to protect
Build a bridge, not a gate

Who put you in command?
Of our water and our land?
If you want to lend a hand
Build a bridge across the Rio Grande[9]

Meanwhile, Tony Drewry's more pointed and caustic "Chinga Tu Muro (Fuck Your Wall)" takes on everything from environmental and social considerations to the historically close relationship between Texas and Mexico to our current fractured national political climate:

There's things in this world that I'll never understand
Like how the hell you're gonna draw a line in the middle
*   of the Rio Grande*

That muddy river flows and it changes every day
And it don't really matter what that Fox News say

It don't make no sense why you'd build this fuckin' fence
Ooh fuck yer wall

Lots of people think that it's all true
That our borders are all unsecure and they're comin' for
 you
Insecure is probably more the case
Now I'm singing this song to the rest of the human race

It don't make no sense why we'd build this fuckin' fence
Ooh fuck yer wall

Think about them bears and them panthers, too
And the animal coyotes doing what they do
If you build a wall that no one can cross
You start a chain reaction of species loss

We better stand up for their rights while we've got time to
 fight
Ooh fuck yer wall

Now there's an angry Cheeto up in Washington
And he's making lots of choices that sound good to him
Just because he says 'em that don't make 'em true
If you think about it long and hard you'll know what to do

Stand up for your rights and never give up the fight
Ooh fuck yer wall

Now Mexico and Texas, well, they've always been
Long before some people made up names for them
And to think we think we own them, well, it kind of
 makes me laugh
Because Mother Nature, well, she always bats last

Stand up for your rights and never give up the fight
Cause it don't make no sense why we'd build this fuckin'
 fence

Ooh fuck yer wall
Ooh fuck yer wall[10]

While the Voices festival inevitably took on new layers of meaning for many participants during the Trump era, others express concern that the festival's future might be threatened if the event becomes too overtly politicized or receives too much national or international exposure. "From the beginning I've worried about that," said Cynta de Narvaez. "But am I worried that there's gonna be a wall put through Big Bend? No, I am not. They've got so many thousands of miles to put in a wall, this is *not* one of those top places *at all*. It's just ridiculous."

Collie Ryan, one of the event's organizers since its inception, agrees. "Voices is *not* going to open the border," she admitted. "We'll make a statement just for the spirit of it. And we don't want it to get bigger and bigger and call that success, because then it's not the right spirit. It's kind of dicey what we're doing, and it's got to be the right spirit to do it. If we keep it smaller, it won't attract so much attention and it can keep going. If it made too much of a statement, there might be energy to put it down. It's best to make no target of ourselves."

Others expressed concern that if Voices became too much of an anti-Trump protest, rather than a protest of the closure of the Lajitas crossing in 2002, the festival would lose support from some of the more politically conservative members of the community. It might be hard to imagine that anyone could consider themselves both a supporter of Trump *and* a supporter of reopening the border in the Big Bend. For a number of Terlingua residents, however, those positions are not in conflict. "There's a guy in town who still flies a confederate flag," Sha Reed Gavin pointed out. "And the thing he's the *most* passionate about is getting this border reopened. People in my experience don't really become invested in something until it touches their life. When it touches your life, like it's touched everybody's lives down here, it becomes real."

I spoke with several Terlingua residents who identified as Trump supporters, and all of them said they support the Voices From Both Sides festival and its message that the Big Bend's unofficial crossings need to be reopened. In fact, while much of the same political polarization that exists in the rest of the country is also present in Terlingua, in all the time I spent there I didn't come across a single person who expressed a belief that the Big Bend needs a wall. How each person reconciles these beliefs varies from individual to individual. "That's only a conflict in other peoples' minds," said one such person. "They have a preconceived notion of how supporting Voices and supporting Trump are in conflict. But those two coincide." Some Trump supporters in the Big Bend insist that when Trump said "wall," he did not necessarily mean a literal, physical wall, but could have instead opted for increasing technology or "boots on the ground" along the border. Others suggest that border security is a priority for them, and that the border in other places might need a wall even if the Big Bend does not. Several people cited the public comments of former US Representative Will Hurd (R-TX), who stated categorically that building a wall through the Big Bend would be costly and unnecessary and who introduced legislation to that effect. Others simply don't believe Trump's rhetoric about the border—"He just *talks*," one person told me—but still chose to support him for other reasons.

"It's been my experience that people vote their wallet," observed Sha. "There are ranchers and people down here who would open that border in a heartbeat. They would keep the pipelines out in a heartbeat. So, yeah, there are some great people here at Voices who I know are Trump supporters, and that's not what this is about for them because they were here when our border got closed."

I cannot say categorically that every Terlingua resident wants the border reopened in the Big Bend. However, I do

believe it is telling, especially when considering how polar-
ized national opinions have become on border issues, that
the overwhelming majority of Terlingua residents, regardless
of political persuasion, want their border crossings reopened,
so that after eighteen long years they might finally again be
able to interact with their neighbors who just happen to live
on the opposite side of a shallow stretch of water.

SHARING SPACE, SHARING CULTURE

As of this writing, I have attended five of the seven Voices
From Both Sides festivals that have occurred to date. While
walking along the banks of the Rio Grande each year, watching children play in the river and listening to musicians on
either side as they take turns singing back and forth, I am always deeply moved by the community solidarity on display.
I have witnessed powerful gestures of friendship and have
heard about many more: next-door neighbors hugging in the
Rio Grande after more than a decade apart; a local sheriff's
deputy helping an elderly woman across the river so she
could meet her grandchildren for the first time; a priest serving communion to people from both countries while knee-
deep in the muddy water; huge families wearing matching
pink t-shirts so they can spot one another across the Rio
more easily. I watched as the Mexican attendees seemed to
grow more comfortable with each passing year. In 2013 and
2014, the traffic wading across the river resembled that at
the new high-tech border crossing at Boquillas: it flowed
mostly one way, with Americans eagerly wading into Mexico but their southern neighbors clearly hesitant to follow
suit. You could hardly blame them for being cautious, what
with the US Border Patrol agents camped high on the hill
overlooking the river, their semi-automatic rifles slung like
banners across their chests.

In later years, the character of the festival began to change.
To their credit, the Border Patrol eventually seemed to

Conjunto La Furia Norteña performs on the Texas bank at the Voices From Both Sides festival, 2018.

realize that the event posed no threat to American national security or sovereignty, and gradually their presence—while never disappearing entirely—started to become less imposing. Mexican attendees began to cross the river in greater numbers, their confidence visibly growing with each successive year that Voices went off without a hiccup. In 2018, there occurred what felt like a huge watershed moment. After several hours playing on the Mexican bank, Conjunto La Furia Norteña waded across the river, their instruments carried safely over their heads, and performed their first set of music in Texas since the border was shut down sixteen years earlier. The crowd was absolutely ecstatic. Many of those present could remember the days when the family band from San Carlos would cross the river to play in Terlingua, and as La Furia launched into their first song, the crowd danced and cheered with the unrestrained enthusiasm of people making up for too many lost years. In all my time in Terlingua,

I don't recall ever seeing a group of musicians more warmly received.

These are the kinds of experiences that make Voices From Both Sides such a memorable event. However, I realized something else while walking along the water's edge, something that surprised me considering Terlingua's proximity to the US-Mexico border. The social integration that makes the festival so powerful—Mexicans and Americans making music together, brown people and white people dancing together to a familiar tune, Spanish and English lilting with equal frequency through the air—that kind of integration does not happen very often in Terlingua during the rest of the year.

According to US Census estimates for 2015, roughly one-third of the population of South Brewster County is Hispanic or Latino/a, but you wouldn't know it from hanging out in the Ghost Town, where the social scene on most days consists almost entirely of Anglo-Americans.[11] Everyone I spoke with during my time in South County expressed a love of the region's multicultural makeup, as well as a sense of solidarity with residents in Paso Lajitas, San Carlos, and other nearby small towns south of the border. These professions of commonality have always struck me as deeply sincere, and while I have never seen any reason to doubt them, one fact remains inescapable: with few exceptions, such sentiments do not seem to play a major role in shaping everyday social life in Terlingua.

I must admit I did not expect this. I had assumed that Terlingua's proximity to the border and its historical relationship with communities on the other side of the river would naturally mean that Mexican-Americans and Anglo-Americans, Spanish speakers and English speakers would interact on a regular basis. In reality, someone spending all their time in the Ghost Town could be forgiven for believing that the Terlingua population is almost entirely Anglo. I asked Terlinguans about this often. Of all the topics I brought up during my many conversations with Terlingua residents, local Anglo/Hispanic relations was the subject with the least amount of consensus. Some longtime residents of South Brewster County suggested that Terlingua used to feel more integrated back when the population was much smaller and the overall sense of community was stronger. "There's a certain gringo population that have been out here long enough that they recognize the Mexicans as *la gente* [the people]," said Ted Arbogast, who moved to Terlingua full-time in 1995. "We're all just the same population. And I guess you just have to be here for a length of time, you know, living in your adobe hut and drinking beer before you see it. There was a certain point in time where it felt like I wasn't a gringo exactly. It was just all of us together. But maybe that's happening less now."

Some long-term residents believe that Terlingua was never truly integrated. "I can't explain it," said Charlotte Teer, who moved to South Brewster County in 1981. "It's just the way it is. The culture here has not quite melded. Or maybe this just *is* the culture. If somebody needs help, the help is there. Otherwise, in normal everyday interactions it's just, 'Hey.' 'Hey.' It's not necessarily bias, just . . . comfort? I don't know." I told Charlotte that, after seeing how strongly people feel about Voices From Both Sides, I had been surprised that the tangible camaraderie that is so evident at the festival is not a more obvious aspect of daily life during the rest of the year. Her response hinted at something important: that the international border is not the only boundary at play in Terlingua. "Voices is a celebration of sharing space," she replied. "*Space* is the word, rather than culture. It is a celebration of opening the gateway, so that you may come over here and I may go over there, because this is one town with a river running through it. But it's two different neighborhoods, and that's the same whether we go over there or they come over here. But it's still one town, and these folks will stand together like you wouldn't believe."

I heard a lot of explanations for why a social gap exists between Terlingua's Mexican and Anglo residents. One obvious reason why the Ghost Town's social and musical scene is predominantly Anglo is that it is centered in bars and other establishments where drinking is prevalent and encouraged. On one hand, Terlingua's Anglo residents include a large number of single adults, retirees, and couples without kids—all demographic groups that frequent the Ghost Town. Terlingua's Mexican population, on the other hand, is overwhelmingly made up of families with children, and very few families or people under the age of twenty-one—regardless of ethnicity—spend regular time in the Ghost Town. Indeed, were it not for my weekly visits to assist with the school band, I could have easily spent my entire two years in Terlingua completely ignorant of the number of children living in the area (notably, the school's student body is majority Hispanic).

One person who has spent his entire life in the area (and who lived across the river in Paso Lajitas before the border was closed) pointed out that the region's Mexican *frontera* (borderlands) culture is highly family-oriented, with priority given to achieving upward economic mobility. "Their number-one goal is to provide better lives for their families," he observed. By contrast, much of the local Anglo population has consciously *eschewed* upward mobility by leaving urban areas and moving to the remote desert—more than one such person referred to this as taking the "Terlingua vow of poverty."

"Generally speaking, this town is two separate communities," observed Cynta de Narvaez, who moved to Terlingua in the mid-1990s. "One is mostly very educated, single, with . . . I won't say a great disrespect for money, but without it being a central force in their lives. And they are from a whole other world. They've *chosen* to be here. But those in the other community [referring to the Mexican population] are married. They have kids. Both parents work. They go shopping in Odessa. They buy new trucks. And many of the adults don't have more than a fifth-grade education. And so you have a huge wall in three or four different areas, and we're not even *talking* about the language barrier yet."

It must be acknowledged that the ability to consciously opt out of financial security in favor of a life in the remote desert—to be able to say "I could be making lots of money in Dallas, but I choose to live here instead"—is an inherently privileged position that is simply not available to most of Terlingua's Hispanic residents. I expect that, were you to take two otherwise identical groups of people, with the same cultural background and the same spoken language at home, and place them side-by-side in a small town, you would likely see much the same kinds of social division that you see in Terlingua today. All this is to say that Anglo Terlinguans and Hispanic Terlinguans are often approaching life in Terlingua with two very different goals in mind. It is perhaps inevitable that these differences would be reflected in local interactions, regardless of ethnicity or national origin.

While people disagree about the extent to which the Anglo and Hispanic populations of Terlingua were ever truly socially integrated, there is a general consensus that the situation has probably gotten worse over the years rather than better. Most of the people I spoke with who were present in South Brewster County to witness the 2002 raid told me that the closure had a profound effect on the social life and integration of the town. Significantly, the closure appears to have had much further-reaching consequences for Terlingua than the seemingly straightforward "splitting of a single community into two." For one, it seems to have also played a role in diminishing the percentage of Spanish speakers among Terlingua's Anglo population. Prior to 2002, fluency in Spanish was fairly common in South County, but today there is a dramatic difference in Spanish fluency between those who lived in Terlingua before the border closure and those who have moved there since. "There's just not that many bilingual people anymore," said Collie Ryan, whose instrumental role in organizing the Voices festival was due in part to her own fluency in Spanish. "Because they're not right there together, there's no incentive to learn a little bit more of the language all the time."

Jim Keaveny, a full-time Terlingua resident since 2009, also believes that the border closure has undermined integration efforts in South County. "Time's a changin'," he said. "I was actually here before 9/11, and I went across to Santa Elena before all that bullshit occurred, which is what it is, bullshit. I'll tell you right now that there was more intermingling. This would be a whole different place if that never stopped. It would be a way better place if they never closed the border. I just think shit like 9/11 and the borders closing, where we can't fuckin' engage with each other, is just screwing everything up even worse. I mean, we already had our challenges where we're trying to learn each other's languages and stuff like that. They're tryin' to learn English, we're tryin' to learn Spanish, we're doin' Spanglish, *la idioma de frontera* [border dialect]. And then that fucked it up even worse 'cause now all the border crossings are closed except for the major border crossings like Presidio and Laredo. I think if we lived in a freer world with less border restrictions, we'd probably be mixing up a lot more on the border."

While most Terlinguans agree that some kind of social divide exists between Anglo and Mexican residents, it was a subject that a lot of locals seemed uncomfortable talking about. On occasions when I brought up the topic, it sometimes felt as if I was exhuming a skeleton in the closet that most people would rather leave unaddressed. With few exceptions, Anglo residents of Terlingua profess a deep sense of solidarity and goodwill toward their Mexican neighbors on both sides of the border, and in all my interactions, I never found any reason to doubt the sincerity of these professions. However, the apparent disconnect between expression and execution—between declarations of solidarity and the reality of how these feelings actually play out in daily life—seems to threaten Terlingua's image of itself as a socially open and inclusive place.

Why the disconnect? Why aren't the feelings expressed at Voices more apparent in how Anglo and Mexican residents of Terlingua interact during the rest of the year? While the factors cited above—the language barrier, upward versus downward mobility, the prevalence of alcohol in the Ghost Town—are certainly part of the equation, I believe there is another factor at play, one that has also shaped my own experience as a native West Texan.

I grew up in Midland, Texas, a politically conservative oil town about four hours from the border with a sizeable Hispanic population. Although my life was full of opportunities to speak Spanish, I never learned the language growing up. Midland was like many towns across the country, segregated in practice if not by law. Anglo Midlanders and Hispanic Midlanders each had their own churches, their own grocery stores, their own neighborhoods and neighborhood schools. In the slice of Midland in which I was raised, fluency in Spanish seemed neither greatly valued nor particularly necessary. I recall overhearing at a young age as adults in my corner of Midland spoke with anxiety about a hypothetical future when English speakers would be "outnumbered in their own state."

As I entered adulthood and began developing an interest in social and cultural traditions different from my own, I began to feel an acute sense of guilt that I had grown up so near the border without learning basic conversational Spanish. Even today my Spanish remains broken at the best of times, and whenever I am attempting to converse with someone in the language, I can't help but feel that I have somehow failed to live up to my end of the implicit social bargain that comes with living in the borderlands. Such feelings often cause me to draw inward whenever a language barrier exists, to become more reserved in my interactions because I am embarrassed by my own inability to communicate the way I wish I could. I can only imagine how my hesitation must appear to the people on the other side of such interactions. It would be all too easy for them to read my reserve and interpret it as disinterest, or mistrust, or even as outright dislike. And who could blame them, especially when considering how much divisiveness exists in our country today regarding language and ethnic diversity? How could I ever expect them to look at me, a gringo from a conservative oil town, and know how I am feeling? How could they possibly intuit that my hesitation comes from the fact that I want to communicate *more*, not less?

I believe that, deep down, many of Terlingua's current Anglo residents feel the same way. Most have moved to Terlingua since 2002 and were never fortunate enough to experience life in the Big Bend when the border was open. The majority of these newer arrivals to the borderlands do not speak Spanish, and they may have difficulty figuring out how to express community sentiment across a cultural and linguistic divide. It is perhaps inevitable that misunderstandings would arise. Unfortunately, the political climate in the United States only serves to exacerbate such misunderstandings. Walls divide, it's true, but so do words, and everyone living along the US-Mexico border is acutely aware of the rhetoric used by America's leaders about the inherent untrustworthiness of Mexican people. By creating an environment of uncertainty and suspicion—in which Mexicans and Anglo Americans are pitted against one another on opposing sides of an eternal struggle and in which immigrants are treated as inherently suspicious at best and inhuman at worst—President Trump and his acolytes have shaped how people in the borderlands interact with one another in real and tangible ways. I can only imagine what it must be like to be a Hispanic person today coming into contact with an Anglo stranger, inevitably wondering *what does this person believe? What do they think about me? Do they find me untrustworthy because of the color of my skin or the language I speak at home?* Of course, for the Anglo person in such interactions, a parallel set of questions arises: *What do they think about me? Do they assume I am afraid of them, that I find them untrustworthy? That I am bigoted or prejudiced because of the color of my skin? How do I convince them I am not what they see on the news?*

Like it or not, this is the environment that exists all along the US-Mexico border today, including in the Big Bend region. While Voices From Both Sides may predate the Trump presidency, it does not occur in a vacuum, and today the festival can only be interpreted in light of our current political moment. When I take a step back and look at all the elements of this story—the Big Bend border's historical fluidity, the 2002 closure and its transformation of social life in the region, Terlingua's long-standing ethnic and linguistic diversity, the joy expressed by local residents as they greet their neighbors in the river, the national political discourse that colors it all—I begin to see that the differences between the Voices From Both Sides festival on one hand, and everyday Anglo/Hispanic interactions in Terlingua on the other, do not represent a disjuncture at all. In the end, Voices is not an expression of how Terlingua *is*. It is an expression of how Terlingua *aspires* to be. In a time of profound social and cultural division in the borderlands, such aspirations have become more important than ever.

ONE FINAL POINT bears discussing at the conclusion of this chapter. Whether they believe that Terlingua used to be more socially integrated or that Terlingua has always consisted of two overlapping communities, most longtime residents seem to agree on one thing: the times when Terlingua feels most like a single, unified community are when people are dancing. As Bill Ivey and Collie Ryan recounted earlier, dances at the Lajitas Trading Post were once a major feature of social life in the lower Big Bend, and residents from miles in every direction would attend. However, most of those dances featured musicians who had crossed the river from Paso Lajitas. In the years since the closure, it has proven prohibitively difficult to bring these groups from Mexico to perform in South County.

"If I could get a band out of Ojinaga, or out of San Carlos, and it wasn't just a pain in the freakin' ass to get them here with all the hoops and the red tape, I would do it," said Buckner Cooke, who was responsible for booking music at the Starlight during my time in the Big Bend. A few years ago, Buckner tried to secure legal passage for Conjunto La Furia Norteña to perform in Terlingua. His efforts proved fruitless. "I got close last year with being able to bring in a band from San Carlos," he said. "Cynta and I worked out a deal with customs, and like two weeks before, customs pulled the deal that would allow them to come over. . . . It all was gonna be worked out, and then suddenly the rug's pulled out from underneath us and we haven't been able to make any headway. So we're being stopped by Homeland Security. By fear."

I have heard a number of Terlinguans lament the fact that there is not more dance music being performed in their town. Although the singer-songwriter music that is prevalent in Terlingua today is perhaps better at encouraging participation among the performers, it does not excel at fostering participation among the audience in the same way that dance music does. This is particularly true where a language barrier exists, as is the case in Terlingua. Whereas singer-songwriter music is primarily a lyrically driven style, dance music needs no translation.

This has been clearly evident at all of the Voices From Both Sides events I have attended, and it is something that Bucker also noticed. "It's an *amazing* event," he said, "but it's the dichotomy of the event that is so interesting. We have our local musicians up there playing, and everyone's standing around, marveling at the fact that this is happening. 'What a great event, this is so awesome, I'm just so happy

I'm here.' And then our musician stops, and then the band on the Mexican side starts, and you just can't help yourself, and suddenly you're in the river and you're dancing and everybody is dancing, and the energy has just *risen*. And there's nothing wrong with our musicians, but as soon as it's our turn, the energy kind of falls down. Nobody's saying, 'Oh, this sucks.' We're just taking a breath and we're going, 'Man, I'm just so happy this is happening, this is just incredible, I cannot believe . . .' And then our local musician stops and the other band starts, and all of a sudden you realize you're dancing again and you're back in the river. I was so struck by that at the first Voices. I was there to take pictures and document the event, and before I realized what was happening, I was in the river dancing."

In the decades since Terlingua's rebirth, one local band has done more to bridge the culture barrier than perhaps any other. Tellingly, they are one of the only groups in Terlingua's history that has consistently performed Mexican music. Los Pinche Gringos (which loosely translates as "The Fucking White Guys") was founded in the early 1990s by a quartet of local musicians: Ted Arbogast on lead guitar and keyboards, Mike Davidson on rhythm guitar, Laird Considine on bass, and Ian Sanchez on drums. According to Mike, the band's creation was inspired by the musicians who once crossed the river at Lajitas to perform for dances at the Trading Post. "I think one of the motivations was that I really like Mexican music," he said. "I'd lived down here, and I really liked goin' to those Mexican dances. After the Rafters [another local band] fell apart, me and Ted started thinkin', *you know, we really need to get us a Mexican band together*. And so we had some cassettes that we wanted to learn some songs on, so we got this waiter at the hotel to write the words down for us, and we started learning some of those tunes."

The bulk of the band's early rehearsals were spent with Sanchez coaching the other members on how to properly pronounce and phrase the words. Eventually, their repertoire expanded to include a wide range of styles, with country and classic rock supplementing a backbone of Mexican cumbia and norteño. According to their website, "the band grew out of the compelling rhythms of the Texas-Mexico border: conjunto, cumbia and all their related offshoots . . . . It is not only that the gringos who have moved to the border during the last 30 years love the spirit of Latino music, we have found that our southern neighbors and Tejano friends also love classic rock and country. The Pinche Gringos have developed a unique synthesis between the music we heard and played as kids, and the music that we eagerly adopted after we migrated to the Big Bend of the Rio Grande."

Laird remembers the band's first gig at La Kiva well. "We were billed as the Pinche Gringos," he recalled, "and the Terlingua Moon wouldn't even print our name 'cause it was offensive. And the Mexicans did show up out of curiosity to see what the heck this was all about. It was just such a mixture . . . the idea was to create a space that embraced this whole trans-border culture here. And I think we started something."

Other Terlingua residents agreed with Laird. "When the Pinche Gringos used to play, we mixed," said Cynta de Narvaez. "Everybody *loved* having the Pinche Gringos play and have *everybody* come and be there. You know, a Mexican man dancing with his wife, and the baby in her arms, and the kid hangin' onto his legs, and they're all dancing in a slow thing together. But this community does not dance anymore. If there was more dance music, everybody would come together again."

Ted Arbogast also remembers that the Pinche Gringos played a major role in creating a social atmosphere that was shared by both Mexican and Anglo residents of South Brewster County. "I loved being able to start the Pinche Gringos and bring the Hispanic Terlingua together with the gringo Terlingua," he said. "I mean, we really did kind of coalesce in those early years, in those early dances, gringo and

Hispanic Terlingua came together. When I got here, I don't think the gringo population and the Mexican population commingled a bunch. I didn't see it. But then the Pinches got together and the word started to get out, and everyone just started coming out. Old Mexicans, young Mexicans, old gringos, dropout gringos. We had a great time. They showed us their dances. And the gringos got together because there's nobody to dance to around here. So it was great. We would play corrido after corrido and they loved it."

I had several opportunities to perform with Los Pinche Gringos during my time in Terlingua, and what I witnessed leads me to believe everything that people said about the role they once played in integrating the town. A few weeks after I arrived in South County, I sat in with the band at a performance in Study Butte (notably, the gig was not in a bar, so more families were present), and the crowd they drew was one of the most diverse I witnessed during my two years of research. At the second annual Voices From Both Sides festival in 2014, someone called across the river on the PA system to invite the Pinches to wade across the river to play their set, thus repeating what had occurred spontaneously the year before. The band did cross, and the energy that their performance inspired in the integrated crowd of Mexican and American dancers was electrifying. Carrying my saxophone across the Rio Grande to perform with the Pinche Gringos was one of the highlights of my time in the Big Bend and one of the most memorable performances of my musical career.

ULTIMATELY, THE SUCCESSES of the Pinche Gringos, the dances at the Lajitas Trading Post, and the Voices festival demonstrate that music can help to foster that sense of community-wide social unity that many residents believe is missing in Terlingua life. Whether it reclaims something that was lost when the border was closed or it creates something entirely new, Voices From Both Sides has provided a space in which Anglo and Mexican residents of the lower Big Bend can come together to celebrate a binational sense of community that sets them apart in twenty-first-century America.

"There is an interest through this Voices From Both Sides," said Collie. "It's allowing a lot of people, like a lot of Mexican people from our side are coming, too. And it allows both races to mix together. And you know what I noticed, when you have a party and both races are there mixing? There's a particular happiness, an upper that happens, that's unique and really nice. This is part of healing."

For now at least, reopening the Lajitas crossing still seems like an impossible dream. For Collie and her neighbors, this is precisely why Voices From Both Sides is so important. In this time of profound division, for one day each year the river has become a unifier once again.

CHAPTER 5

GETTING FATTER

*When I first walked down those dusty, silent
streets and peered into the darkened mining shafts,
I sensed the presence of another age. I wanted to
know the people who transformed that barren waste
into a prosperous industrial community, where they
came from, how they lived. . . . Today little remains
of the Chisos Mining Company installations at
Terlingua to indicate its once vital past. The people
are all gone. The old company store, the abandoned
jail, the slowly decaying Perry mansion, and the vacant adobe ruins are its only testaments to the past.
Terlingua is a ghost town.*
—KENNETH BAXTER RAGSDALE, *Quicksilver*, 1976

WHEN HISTORIAN Kenneth Baxter Ragsdale penned the
above words as part of what would become the definitive
history of Terlingua's mining period, he likely could not
have imagined the process that was about to begin in the
tiny deserted town that was his subject. The first intrepid
river guides moved into the Ghost Town the year after Ragsdale's book was published. More than four decades later, Terlingua bears little resemblance to the abandoned site that he
described. The old company store is now a souvenir shop,

and the abandoned jail has been converted into restrooms for the nearby Starlight Theatre Restaurant & Bar. On the hill overlooking the town, the Perry Mansion has been refurbished, and its rooms are available to rent for tourists seeking an unconventional lodging experience. When walking along the main road—paved now, but still dusty—a person might hear the prevailing silence broken by a string of passing cars on the highway, or by the faint sounds of a guitar or a singer's voice floating lazily off the Porch through the dry desert air. Most of the vacant adobe ruins that Ragsdale saw as he ambled through the town are no longer vacant; once the makeshift homes of miners, the majority have been refashioned into affordable housing for a new era of Terlingua residents whose numbers grow with each passing year. Terlingua is no longer a ghost town in the conventional sense. It is a ghost town reborn.

Although South Brewster County has not yet regained its peak population from World War I, more than forty years of continuous growth have transformed the area dramatically in the lifetimes of the people who live there. Once an all-but-forgotten curiosity along a remote stretch of highway, notable primarily for its proximity to one of the less frequented national parks, the Terlingua Ghost Town has since become an attraction in itself. Where once the town was mentioned only in passing as a place to eat or sleep en route to other points of interest, recent write-ups in *Texas Highways*, *Texas Monthly*, and the *New York Times* now extol the virtues of Terlingua as a quirky travel destination in its own right. A bustling vacation rental economy has sprung up in the past several years to accommodate this growing interest, creating more income streams for local residents while also stoking fears that Terlingua is losing its sense of self. Meanwhile, the town's increased exposure to the outside world has led to a new influx of permanent residents, most of whom have been attracted to the Big Bend by the promise of a small-town desert life that, given Terlingua's growth, seems more and more fleeting with each passing year.

Terlingua's identity has long been predicated on its differentness. The eastern sunsets, the campfire jams, the isolation in a singular desert environment, the lagging modern infrastructure, the tiny population, the historically fluid international border, the deep sense of community—these are the essential traits that give the town its character, those irreducible qualities that make Terlingua *Terlingua*.[1] What happens, then, if these qualities disappear? This is the question on many local residents' minds whenever they talk about the changes that have shaped their town in recent years. To be fair, some longtime Terlinguans are sick of the subject. They correctly point out that things like population growth and developing infrastructure have always been part of life in Terlingua. Others, however, believe that the pace of change has increased in recent years, and that the town might be on its way to a tipping point. The fluid border is already a thing of the past, and campfire-style jams may be inching toward the same fate. What will be the next domino to fall?

GETTING FATTER

"Picture the Ghost Town," said Laird Considine, gesturing as if giving me his own personal tour of the past. "When you turn into the Ghost Town, it's still a dirt road. There's no High Sierra right there on the right, there's none of Herman's stuff right behind that. There's no vet and all of his mess over here, there's no pirate ship or Jimmy's stuff goin' on over there. There's *nothin'*. No Terlingua Ghost Town Café, none of these other little trailers, no Ed's place, none of that stuff going on. There's no art gallery, no Posada Milagro up on the hill. You get up the road a bit and there's the jail cell where the restrooms are now, and then there's the Starlight Theatre, which had just opened as a restaurant when I moved here."

Laird moved to Terlingua in 1992 when the town was only a fraction of its present size. From where the two of us sat in my trailer drinking beer, the Starlight was only a few hundred yards up the road. If we looked out the window, we could see the glow of neon lights illuminating the building's entrance.

"Next to the Starlight is the Far Flung office," Laird said, continuing his memory tour. "When you pass the Boathouse Restaurant, back then it was the Far Flung boathouse. And there's the Terlingua Trading Company. Around behind it there was the Holiday Hotel where a bunch of people lived for $50 or $100 a month. Now it's a fancy place. The Perry Mansion was totally in ruins, and where the crisis center is now, there was a much smaller building where Pam Ware had her restaurant. And that was it. Now, I drive up the road and I go, 'God, this is *ugly*. This is like . . . blight.'" Laird took a swig of beer and looked down at the table. "That was part of the charm," he went on. "Back when it was just a little ghost town up a dirt road off the highway, and there was pretty much nothing there. The cemetery, a couple ruins, and that was about it. It certainly wasn't for everybody. And there were people who had already been here for *twenty years* before I got here. Imagine how frustrating all the changes must be to them. There was no power grid going hardly anywhere, no community water system, no . . . well, you've heard 'Getting Fatter.'"

Laird wrote "Getting Fatter" while I was living in Terlingua as an ode to the town he has called home for nearly thirty years. Its title holds a clever double meaning, marking the passage of time and the onset of older age while also alluding to Terlingua's growth. It is at turns funny, nostalgic, and sad, written from the perspective of a person who has watched his town change before his eyes, and who can't be entirely sure whether his response to the change is justified or if he is simply being crotchety. The song captures a lot of ambivalence, a complex emotion that is tricky to capture succinctly in verse. There is a recognition of the ephemeral nature of idyllic small town life coupled with a wistful acceptance of such a life's impermanence. It poignantly captures how many longtime residents feel when reflecting on Terlingua's growth through the years.

Several verses into the song, Laird begins listing many of the new developments he has witnessed during his three decades in Terlingua. His rapid-fire delivery, punctuated in the middle by a sigh, conveys a sense of bewilderment at how quickly the town has changed.

> Well, our little town, it's grown so rapidly
> I hardly know who all to thank
> For the high school and the water system and the
>   emergency services
> And the community center and the hardware store and the
>   [breathes a sigh]
> General store and the party barn and the Church of Christ
> And the drive-through liquor and uh,
> Oh yeah, the pirate ship and there's a brontosaurus now on
>   the highway
> And uh, who all am I forget—oh, and of course the bank![2]

Significantly, all of the new businesses and services that Laird references would have required a 160-mile round-trip to Alpine not long ago, and their availability in South County today has made living in the lower Big Bend much easier than it once was. "I suggest that every advance in technology creates a new wave of population that all of a sudden can handle living in the desert," opined Far Flung founder Mike Davidson.

Bryn Moore, who has lived in Terlingua since the mid-1980s, agreed. "I think the change started accelerating when we got a water system," she said. "All of the sudden, people are thinking, *Oh, I can be just as comfortable as I am in Dallas.* And now people are becoming more open to using solar power and water catchment, so that opens up land that used to be really empty and protected to a lot more building. I think that's where the changes are going to happen the most. They already have."

Several longtime residents told me that a seismic surge in population seemed to occur when satellite TV and internet became available in Terlingua. The introduction of such in-home technologies had a significant effect on the social life of the town by making it easier for people to stay at home rather than leaving the house to find entertainment. Residents say the makeup of the town's population has changed now that amenities and conveniences have made living in the desert more feasible for a wider variety of people. "I'd say 80 percent of the people that you see around town everyday couldn't have existed under those early circumstances," said Mike Davidson.

Laird agreed. "It's always been a magnet for certain kinds of souls, and I think that's going away," he told me. "Now it's grown enough that it's becoming a magnet for people who would not have fit in or been attracted here twenty-five years ago. There's still plenty of land out here, and there's a lot of people in the cities who want to get away and who have enough money to build nice places with big solar collections and big water catchments, and who want to live off the grid in a much fancier way than hanging the shower bag from the corner of the roof and standing out there naked, waving at your neighbors as they drive by."

Ted Arbogast, who moved to Terlingua in the mid-1990s and who now runs Studio Butte recording studio, echoed Laird's comments, saying that class divisions among the population are more noticeable today. "The up-and-up strata of society is starting to be here that wasn't here," he said. "There's almost an upper class in Terlingua now. It felt like that didn't happen before. I suppose there were still owners of everything back then, but it was almost like it was a communal thing and everybody owned it more or less. It just seemed a lot freer. There was no ownership, only sharing. Of kind of everything."

One of the most eloquent observers of Terlingua's growth is Paul Wiggins, whose move to the lower Big Bend predates that of even the earliest river guides. "This was a hard place to live in 1968," he told a writer for *Outside Magazine* in 2014. "You had to figure out where the other human beings were and how to get along with them. Now it's turned into kind of a scene. The mainstream is getting closer, it's getting easier to be here, and that's changing the place, bringing the best and worst of what dense human society has to offer. We're a little unprepared for that."[3]

Regardless of when they moved to the desert, almost everyone in Terlingua agrees that population growth in South Brewster County is inevitable. However, the growth itself is not what concerns most residents. As more and more people move to Terlingua who would never have considered living there several decades ago, many longtime Terlinguans are worried that their town will begin to resemble the very places all these new arrivals left behind. "It seems like a lot of people move out here because they love the place, and the first thing they try to do is change it," said one resident who was quoted in a 2014 article in *Texas Monthly*. "They bring parts of the big city that they wanted to leave so bad out here with them."[4] This concern is widely shared among both longtime residents and more recent arrivals.

"For the longest time I think people here were fine with going 80 miles one way to the doctor," said Anna Oakley, who moved from Austin to Terlingua in 2009. "And most of us are still fine with that. But the more people we get from big cities who aren't happy without having those luxuries, they're going to want it to change, and then they will be the majority. That's my fear. It's just like what happened to Marfa."

Marfa is a town of a few thousand people in the upper Big Bend region about two hours northwest of Terlingua. Once notable primarily as a ranching community and railroad stop, in recent decades the town has developed an international reputation as an unlikely capital for the visual arts, thanks in large part to the influence of renowned minimalist Donald Judd, who moved to Marfa from New York City in the early 1970s. In the years since, the town has accommodated—begrudgingly at times—a steadily growing population of New Yorkers and artsy types, and this process has profoundly transformed the character of the town.[5] I heard several Terlingua residents refer to Marfa as a kind of worst-case scenario for what might happen to Terlingua.

"Marfa was this tiny little nothing town," Anna said, "and more people started going there who thought it was quaint and cute. 'Oh, and let's buy this house, and let's buy this.' And all these New Yorkers came, and then they started complaining about the trailers and the chickens and the goats, which is what gave it its charm! And now there's building codes and all these new rules in Marfa. So it's like, what you *moved* there for, you have changed. So that's where I see Terlingua going. I mean, La Posada already has a flush toilet out front! 'Cause it's too hard to tell people from Austin to walk across the parking lot. So you just see things like that, and it's like, *Wow* . . ."

While it might seem trivial to point to a coffee shop's new flush toilet as a sign of Terlingua's growth, Anna's comments are indicative of a much larger trend in local discourse. The individual changes that people identify—a toilet, a bank, the introduction of satellite TV—end up becoming signposts in Terlingua's history that take on much broader meaning. Like the Starlight getting a roof, these iconic moments ultimately serve to symbolize the process of change in Terlingua as a whole.

Practically everyone in Terlingua who talks about change does so using these signposts—indeed, they have become such an important part of local discourse that conversations about change occasionally begin to resemble verses from Laird's song. One Terlingua resident I spoke with recalled with angst how a new neighbor had recently bulldozed a beautiful nearby butte in order to build a house; another mentioned with a hint of sadness the day the Ghost Town road was paved. I heard several longtime locals refer to the "stop sign wars" of the early 1990s, a period when the county government repeatedly tried to erect stop signs at local intersections, and anonymous Terlingua residents, concerned about the urbanization the stop signs apparently represented, repeatedly removed the signs during the night. A number of people mentioned the installation of public water and plumbing, or the opening of the Cottonwood grocery store, or any one in a series of local venues becoming "too touristy." I have even heard new arrivals refer to hypothetical *future* signpost moments. One person who had lived in South County for fewer than five years told me that "when they get an ATM in the Ghost Town, that's gonna make a big difference."

A few residents pointed to a signpost moment that was particularly symbolic for them: local bars banning smoking. "I don't smoke and I've never smoked," said Anna. "But with all the non-smoking ordinances in the state, coming down here for the first time felt so lawless, 'cause you could just walk into a bar and *smoke*. When they changed that I actually put up a fight about it. I was like, 'That's what Terlingua is! It's lawless, man.'"

Jim Keaveny agreed. "It sounds like a really stupid superficial thing to focus on," he said, "but that's kind of almost like a hallmark, you know. It's like, if you can't go into a bar and fuckin' smoke a cigarette . . . . And I'm not sayin' smoking is good or anything. I'm just sayin' there's a certain libertarian freeness about it."

I experienced my own share of signpost moments during my time in Terlingua. Although my residence in the Big

Bend was relatively brief, Terlingua seemed to change so much during that short span that at times it became challenging to write about the town with any consistency. On more than one occasion during the research and writing for this book, I composed a description of a particular musical event or venue, only to find six months later that it no longer existed or was no longer recognizable as I had described it. Two months after my arrival in Terlingua, for example, I wrote a description in my journal of the Boathouse Bar, a Ghost Town bar a few hundred yards down the road from the Starlight. "The Boathouse is as much of a dive on the inside as it appears on the outside," I wrote. "The floor is well-worn concrete covered with dust and splintered wood. An old cast-iron stove sits at one end of the room, with a stack of wooden pallets and empty cardboard for fuel sitting nearby. Polaroid photographs are thumbtacked thickly on the walls. In the center of the room is a partially disassembled motorcycle that is surrounded by tools, rags, and half-empty cans of WD-40. The Boathouse doesn't serve liquor, and its food menu is limited to microwave pizzas and small bags of chips. But the Lone Star is cheap, a buck-fifty a can."

When I wrote the above description, the Boathouse was primarily a locals bar, the kind of place where Terlingua residents could find refuge during the busy season when the other establishments in town were overflowing with out-of-towners. On more than one occasion, I watched as a group of tourists came into the room, took one look around, and left as quickly as they had entered. Of course, for locals hungry for a bit of the old Terlingua vibe, that was precisely the way they liked it.

Three months after my journal entry, news began to spread around town that the Boathouse was closing. New owners who had recently moved to Terlingua were now in the mix, and they wanted to renovate the building and reopen it as a much nicer venue, complete with full kitchen and bar. Not surprisingly, many residents were not pleased. "This town is just changing so damn fast," said one local musician. "First it was the Study Butte Store, then the Ghost Town Saloon, and now the Boathouse." Some people lamented the loss of one of the few social spaces in town still reserved mostly for residents, while others complained that yet another space for informal jams was being converted into a commercial space for gigs.

Individual signpost moments obviously vary a great deal from person to person. Although practically everyone recognizes the broad process of change, each person's perspective on change depends on when they moved to Terlingua and on which elements of Terlingua life they value most. Thus, in his song "Getting Fatter," Laird neglected to mention the Starlight's roof—a major signpost moment for those who lived in Terlingua in the 1970s and 80s—because the roof was already in place when Laird arrived in town. For the same reason, someone writing an analogous song after moving to Terlingua in 2007 would probably not mention the new high school or the public water system. Most Terlinguans would see no symbolic significance in the smoking bans to which Jim and Anna referred, but they might see tremendous significance in the opening of Terlingua's first real grocery store. The thing that unites all these interpretations is this: while each person's individual perspective ultimately shapes which changes they see as significant, the ubiquity of these signpost moments within the local imagination demonstrates that concern about the process of change is not limited to a small group of old-timers or longtime residents, but rather is a topic of consequence for a broad spectrum of Terlinguans regardless of when they arrived.

For most Terlingua residents who express concern about the growth of their town, their greatest fears are not superficial changes like the installation of new utilities, the imposition of new regulations, and the development of once empty land. Above all, they are worried about what population growth will do to the local spirit of community. After all, how large can a town become before it can no longer be considered close-knit? Today, South Brewster County has a year-round population of perhaps five hundred and a winter population that likely approaches two thousand—far too many people to allow for close relationships with all of them. While this might still seem small to most readers, it represents massive growth when considering what the Terlingua area looked like when the first river guides moved into the Ghost Town in the late 1970s. Not surprisingly, longtime Terlingua residents say they have witnessed a decrease in community sentiment as the town has grown.

"I would describe it as tribal," said Bryn Moore when I asked her what Terlingua was like when she moved there in 1985. "There were so few people then, so you really had to cooperate in some sort of tribal fashion for everything. For drinking water, for entertainment, for beer, to get a free burger 'cause you don't have the money to pay till Friday, all of that. It was very tribal. There were usually one or two things a week going on, and everybody would go to whatever was happening. Now, there's just so many more people, it's a lot more . . . I don't like the word 'clique,' but I would say there are more factions now, and more things going on than there were back then. It's not so tribal anymore."

Mark Lewis agreed. "There's a bunker mentality now in some ways," he said. "People hide out at private parties. The public gatherings don't happen as much anymore, and the venues are all bars, so if you don't like hangin' out in a bar then you just don't go out. So if there's any action from the old days happenin' around Terlingua, it's happenin' in somebody's backyard, and you need an invitation to get in."

This slow fracturing of the community is one of the things that inspired Laird Considine to write "Getting Fatter." "There's more little nooks and crannies of community that overlap now," Laird said. "Little different subgroups of community. I don't remember it being quite like that when I first moved here. There was more of a cohesive identity than there is now. And more people makes it . . . different. It used to be that you knew everybody. I mean literally *everybody*. But now I'm always meeting people who say things like, 'Oh yeah, we just bought forty acres out by Hen Egg' and 'I've been living out there for the last . . . .' I met some people on the road while walking my dogs the other day who said, 'You must be one of our neighbors, we bought a place out here a couple years ago.' And I'm thinking to myself . . . '*Neighbors*? I've never seen you before in my life.'"

I failed to see all these "nooks and crannies of community" when I first arrived in Terlingua. Going out almost every evening, I found that it did not take me long to meet most of the people who visited the Ghost Town with any regularity, and I began to assume—naively, it turns out—that by hanging out on the Porch and in the Starlight every day I was developing a fairly representative snapshot of the people who make up the Terlingua community. However, there are plenty of residents of South Brewster County who do not frequent the Ghost Town on a regular basis. Some Terlinguans never go there. A person could spend a decade sitting on the Porch and still never meet all the people who live in South Brewster County.

The Ghost Town might be the center of musical life in Terlingua, but it is not the center of Terlingua life for all residents. Because South County is so large, it takes a long time for some people to get to the Ghost Town—as much as a two-hour round-trip for those living at the area's outlying edges. Several decades ago, when Terlingua's population density was much lower, people were willing to make this trip more often, since the only alternative for many was to sit at home alone. Thanks to new technologies and population growth, however, most people living on Terlingua's margins now have social opportunities much closer to home. Another reason that many residents of South Brewster County do not frequent the Ghost Town is the prevalence of alcohol. The consumption of alcohol is a virtual constant in the

Ghost Town social scene, and this has led to an unfortunate stereotype that the Ghost Town is a haven for drunks. While my own experience has not led me to believe that Terlingua has a higher incidence of alcoholism than anywhere else I've ever lived, public consumption is certainly a routine part of Ghost Town life. As a result, people who wish to avoid places where drinking is prevalent—families with young children, for example—do not often visit the Ghost Town.

Finally, some Terlinguans choose not to frequent the Ghost Town for political reasons, as it is considered by some to be a social center for "hippie," or liberal, Terlingua. While the people who make up the Ghost Town social scene are certainly not exclusively politically left-leaning, I do believe that visitors to Terlingua would get a very different overall impression of its political makeup from visiting the town's more remote outlying areas than they would if they spent all their time in the Ghost Town.[6]

This reveals another fascinating point about South Brewster County: people from polar opposite ends of the ideological spectrum are drawn to the same remote desert environment for sometimes very different reasons. A person moving to Terlingua in order to live off-grid, as a means of reducing her impact on the environment, might have for a neighbor a person who moved to Terlingua in an attempt to free himself from the clutches of what he believes is an overbearing or tyrannical government.

In the end, I realized that, despite its small size, Terlingua is far more diverse and socially complex than it might appear at first glance. In a way, the challenge of capturing the town completely in a single book reflects the very changes that long-term residents note. Twenty or thirty years ago, Terlingua was much more unified, and the music that was being made there was an integral part of *everyone's* lives. Today, however, there are increasingly many different overlapping Terlinguas, and the Ghost Town—where the overwhelming majority of local music still occurs—is only one of these worlds.

Before moving on, I should say that, despite their misgivings, Terlingua residents are acutely aware of the often complicated nature of change in their town, including recognizing their own roles in the process. Most of the people I spoke with freely admitted that by moving to South County they had themselves contributed to the very processes of growth and change that concerned them. Several Terlinguans even alluded to the "observer effect"—a concept in physics stating that the mere act of observing can influence the thing being observed—as a way of describing how their own presence might have contributed to the town's change. Virtually everyone recognizes that going on and on about change can at times seem a bit cliché, that change is a "fact of life" that is ever present, and that each person's perspective on change is determined in large part by when he or she arrived. "It's a standing joke," said Pat O'Bryan. "I mean, everybody wishes they could have slammed the gate shut the minute *they* got here."

Mike Davidson, one of the founders of Far Flung Adventures, agreed. "As far as I'm concerned, it was compromised twenty years ago," he said. "It's just a matter of perspective. Everybody wants to be the last explorer. And I've got as much grounds for bemoaning the changes as anybody. I mean, shit, in the 80s we were the only guys around. But shit changes, and that's just the way it is."

There are positive aspects to Terlingua's growth as well. The construction of a K-12 school in 1997 has been a blessing for high school students in Terlingua, who previously had to endure a 180-mile round-trip—the longest in the United States—in order to attend classes in the next town.[7] Local residents have thus learned to take the good with the bad. "There's things I don't like about the way it's grown," said Bryn Moore, who moved to Terlingua in 1985. "But it's inevitable, and there's a lot of good about what's happened. It used to be you could only buy a brown speckled head of iceberg lettuce if you were *lucky*, so it's nice to have the Cottonwood [grocery store] here. And we've got a school now, and a bank, so that's more convenient. But there will never be stories coming out of this place like there were before all the conveniences and infrastructure was in place. I'm thankful that I was here to see it before things got easier. But I'm not necessarily unhappy that things are easier now."

IF CHANGE IS INEVITABLE, as most Terlinguans seem to agree, what, if anything, is to be done about it? Answers to that question are as varied as the Terlingua population it-self. In recent years, some local residents, concerned by what they believe is an alarming trend of commercialism taking over Terlingua, have taken it upon themselves to make their opinions known in the community. More #NotLikeMarfa bumper stickers are popping up around town now, and one local resident circulated a hand-drawn cartoon on social me-dia decrying the rapid increase in local vacation rentals: a tombstone in the desert with "RIP Old Terlingua" written in the foreground. Around the same time, an anonymous res-ident papered the town with flyers criticizing anyone "rap-idly trying to change Terlingua." The flyer didn't name any names or list any specific grievances, but whoever posted it made his or her opinion about change abundantly clear. "If you don't understand and respect the way of life, the land, the history, and this great community, then you don't belong here. Don't think it's a big deal? How does this affect you, and what's at stake? Everything you love about Terlingua, Texas. Just look at what happened to Marfa."

Other residents believe that, while change might be im-possible to stymie, Terlinguans nevertheless possess the power to shape change in ways that help maintain their town's character and promote it into the future. "Everything changes," said Sha Reed Gavin. "That's what I finally had to come to terms with. Everything changes, so we can either help guide the change with integrity, or we can let it take over and say, 'What the hell happened?'"

Pat O'Bryan agreed. "Terlingua is on a cusp," he said. "Things will never be like they were before. If we work together, we can construct a future for our town and our neighbors that we can all live with."

Since music is such a central element of Terlingua life, it has naturally become one of the primary activities through which Terlingua residents seek to promote their town's identity and community spirit in the face of change. The Voices From Both Sides festival is an obvious example of this, but there are others as well. In recent years, Terlingua musicians began organizing benefit concerts to raise money for local causes. During my time in Terlingua, benefits of this kind occurred roughly once a month, and each one featured numerous local musicians who donated their time and money to perform short sets for an audience of benefactors (tip jars and musicians' fees are also contributed to the fund).

"Once you're in the community," said Jeffro Greasewood, one of the organizers of these events, "you understand that it's a pretty close-knit thing, and everybody helps each other to survive. And musicians are one of the biggest proponents of that. Whenever there's a cause, the musicians around here are always on board. It's one of the big ways of raising money here. Someone says, 'We gotta get some money for so-and-so, how we gonna do it?' 'Well, let's get some music, number one.'"

Local guitarist Pat O'Bryan was also responsible for organizing a number of benefit concerts during my time in Terlingua. As Pat recalls, the benefit concerts developed organically. "I decided I wanted to throw a New Year's Eve party," he said, "so I called up all the usual suspects, and I brought my PA system into the American Legion, and I sort of just ran it loosely. And it was George Goss who pointed out that Collie Ryan had had an injury to her leg, and he said, 'We oughta pass the hat for Collie.' And we did, and we raised a couple hundred bucks. Then one of the Davis [pseudonym] boys got cancer and needed gas money and hotel room money and food money to go get treated in Odessa. Well, we had a benefit, raised money, and were able to pay for that. So word started to get around anytime anyone needed something, and that's how it started."

In the years since the inaugural concert Pat described, these benefits have raised money for a wide range of local causes, among them the Terlingua Community Garden, the community theater, the high school track team, high school music and art programs, the local food bank and family crisis center, the school library (which doubles as the local public library), a number of Terlingua residents dealing with various health issues, Terlingua Fire and EMS services, a local resident and undocumented immigrant who needed help with legal fees, and a summer art school for area children. Because the term "local" in Terlingua historically extends to small towns across the border, money was raised to provide trauma counseling at an orphanage in nearby Ojinaga, Chihuahua, and also to provide tuition for a promising student from Boquillas, Coahuila—one of Terlingua's sister towns on the border—so she could attend high school in Chihuahua City (the Boquillas school goes only through the eighth grade, and students are no longer able to cross the river to attend school in Terlingua).

The significance of these events extends far beyond the money raised. As Pat O'Bryan observed, they provide local musicians with an opportunity to give back to the community in a tangible way—even for those who might not have any money in their pockets to donate. "There's a lot of benefits all the way around," Pat said, "because even if you're a musician and you don't have two nickels to rub together, you can still help someone else. So it's not just the person who gets the money at the end of the night that benefits. Everybody gets that life-affirming feeling of doing something good."

Equally important, however, is that these events deeply reinforce the town's community spirit at a time when Terlingua's growing population and changing social climate have called the future of that spirit into question. "It was amazing to see the show of support for the community," said an attendee at one of the local benefits. "Terlingua is a very awesome place, and not just because it's beautiful. It's also the people: how they have such a sense of each other's needs and how they support one another in ways that lift the spirit like no other place I have ever been. I consider it home and all of you as family."

In the end, the above quote reveals an important lesson about contemporary life in Terlingua that I experienced first-hand: despite how they might appear at the outset, not all changes are negative, nor do they always result in a loss of community. The benefit concert she was referring to was a weekly event that took place in the newly renovated Boathouse Restaurant & Bar, which reopened under new ownership during my time in town and whose initial closure had been such a signpost moment in my own Terlingua experience. Despite fears that the new Boathouse would be too touristy and too commercial, it quickly became the de facto center of the Terlingua music scene and remained so for nearly two years. When the Boathouse eventually closed again in 2016 (it remains closed as of this writing), the party on closing night felt like a wake for a beloved friend, full of speeches, tears, musical performances, and celebrations of the spirit of community that was cultivated there. Among the hundred or so people in attendance were many who had initially been upset about the Boathouse's previous closure and change of management. "The Boathouse proves how a place can 'change' but still maintain the original integrity of a place," said one such person.

DURING MY TIME in Terlingua, I witnessed countless examples of community being cultivated through music making. Some, such as Voices From Both Sides and the benefit concerts mentioned above, have community building as their explicit purpose. Other events, such as open mics at the Boathouse, song circles at La Kiva, and jams on the Porch—events that form the bulk of Terlingua's musical life—create community in subtler ways. This second kind of community building usually goes unstated, but this renders it no less powerful. The deep connections that Terlinguans make with one another through music can be heard in the songs that local residents write about their town, and in Carol Whitney's joyful recounting of her first Porch jam. They reveal themselves in the sadness that residents feel about the loss of campfires and the transformation of local venues. Ultimately, the true importance of Terlingua music is not in the sounds themselves—it is in the relationships that are created in the pursuit of those sounds.

In my two years in Terlingua, no musical event that I witnessed was more profoundly affecting, or demonstrated the community spirit more powerfully, than one that occurred just four months into my tenure. It took place in a parking lot, behind a barrier of police tape on one of the darkest days in Terlingua's history.

Glenn Felts was a larger-than-life character in Terlingua. The owner and operator of La Kiva Restaurant & Bar for twenty-three years, he arrived in the Big Bend in 1991 when his uncle, Gil Felts, passed away. Glenn eventually took over the business that Gil had founded, and he quickly fell in love with the Terlingua lifestyle. For more than two decades, Glenn was a central figure in the local community. As one resident summed it up, if Terlingua had a mayor, Glenn would have been a frontrunner for the position.

As the owner of one of the primary venues in town, Glenn was especially important as a patron of the local music scene. La Kiva was home to what Terlingua residents affectionately referred to as the "longest-running open mic in the world." Whether or not this claim was accurate, La Kiva's unbroken streak of nearly nine hundred consecutive Wednesday open mics was quite an impressive feat. For seventeen straight years, rain or shine, holiday or weekday, the music contin-ued. Even on days when the restaurant was forced to close due to one of the recurring power outages that plague Ter-lingua's shoddy electrical grid, someone would always show up, without fail, to keep La Kiva's open-mic tradition alive.

In the early morning of February 4, 2014, Glenn was found brutally beaten to death outside his La Kiva Restaurant. Later that morning, a local resident—a friend of Glenn's and of many others in the community—was arrested and charged with Glenn's murder. An event like this would be heartbreaking for any small town; most Terlingua residents knew both Glenn and the man charged with his murder, which only made the event doubly excruciating. However, for Terlingua in particular—a place where the spirit of com-munity is held in such high regard—Glenn's murder was truly devastating. Events like this aren't supposed to happen in towns like Terlingua.

The outside world was quick to jump on the story. An article in *Texas Monthly* portrayed Glenn's death as yet an-other sign that Terlingua was changing for the worse.[8] An-other in *Outside Magazine* claimed "the community frac-tured" in the weeks following the event.[9] In a move that most Terlingua residents consider an egregious exploitation of the tragedy, a crew for the National Geographic Channel came to Terlingua to film a reality TV show centered around Glenn's murder. "Glenn was a friend of mine," said Buckner Cooke, echoing the opinions of many others in town. "And how they portray Glenn, we have no control over. And it's gonna play out to the entire nation. If you're gonna tap into Glenn's murder and say that this is Terlingua, and they're gonna get to define what Terlingua is and who we are? Then I got a problem with it. And then you're gonna drag my friend, who was brutally murdered, and you're going to use that for profit? I got an issue with that."

Not surprisingly, most Terlingua residents condemned the television series, although a handful of people did choose to participate. This created divisions within the community that still have not healed. However, while the suggestion that Terlingua's community spirit was compromised by Glenn's tragic death certainly makes for a compelling narrative, that is not at all what I witnessed.

On the day of Glenn's passing, it felt as if every law enforcement official in the Big Bend had suddenly descended upon Terlingua. With a perimeter of yellow police tape surrounding the entire La Kiva property, news of the tragedy spread through town like a wildfire. As the reality of the situation slowly settled on the community, someone pointed out that the following day was scheduled to be La Kiva's 886th consecutive open mic. Everyone agreed that Glenn would not have wanted such a long-running and cherished musical tradition to meet such a tragic end.

Plans were made, and law enforcement was consulted. Early the next afternoon, Terlingua residents began to gather along the highway outside the police perimeter. It was an unusual day in the lower Big Bend, overcast and dreary with a biting wind chill that made it one of the coldest days I experienced during my time in the desert. Residents clustered in small groups on the shoulder of the road, bundled up in layers of infrequently worn jackets and scarves and gloves, waiting. At the appointed time, the sheriff came out to the road and lifted the police tape so that the crowd could pass underneath. We would not be allowed in the building, so instead we crossed the dirt parking lot and gathered in a sheltered spot near La Kiva's famous cave-like entrance.

The fifty or so people in attendance remained mostly silent as the musicians unpacked their instruments and, unamplified, began to play. The music didn't last long—only about a half-hour—and the "stage" wasn't the raucous hive of energy that was typical of most La Kiva open mics. With tears shimmering in their eyes, local songwriters took turns singing original songs about Terlingua, heavy-hearted renditions of songs I had heard performed so joyously so many

A depiction of the open mic in the parking lot following Glenn Felts's death. The painting by Lynn Davis hangs on the wall at La Kiva, 2016.

times before. Their voices cracked, and their instruments were far too cold to play reliably in tune, but it didn't matter. All that mattered was that the community was there. As the refrains of the familiar songs continued, supported by the quirky combination of Ted's mandolin, Moses's harmonica, Crystal's melodica, Mark's washtub bass, and Reed's guiro cheese grater, it felt for the first time since Glenn's death like Terlingua again. Then Alex began the chorus of "79852" and everyone quietly sang along.

GREEN CHILE STEW

IT HAS BEEN almost two years since the bulk of my time in
Terlingua came to an end, and I still think about the town
and its people every day. There is a lot that I miss about
living in the Big Bend. For one thing, I play nowhere near as
much music as I did in Terlingua, where music making was
a daily or even multiple-times-daily occurrence. I will also
forever cherish the sense of community I experienced while
living in the remote desert of West Texas, a spirit the like of
which I have never encountered anywhere else.

However, Terlingua has also been on my mind lately for
other reasons. It seems that every time I log into social me-
dia I'm seeing a new think piece about the weird singularity
of the Terlingua community or yet another write-up in a
travel magazine about the hidden treasures of the lower Big
Bend. When I talk with friends in the area the refrain is often
the same: Terlingua is growing too damn fast.

A few weeks into my tenure in the Big Bend, I was standing on the Porch while watching the sunset paint the Chisos
when a local resident I had gotten to know fairly well approached me from the Starlight's entrance. The two of us had
been talking earlier that day about the attention being given
to Terlingua and the increasing rate at which people seemed
to be moving to the town. The woman stood next to me for

a few minutes as we both looked out over the desert scene. Then, without preamble, she turned to ask me a question.

"What happens when you write your book and tell the world all about Terlingua, and then lots of people read it and suddenly they all want to move here?"

I must admit that the question caught me off guard. At the time, I did not have an answer that felt satisfying. Although she later recanted her objection, the worry in her voice has stayed with me ever since, and I have continued to think about her words in the intervening years. Her question is an important one that deserves to be raised: in a town whose residents are so obviously concerned about being increasingly "on the map," how can I, as a conscientious writer, justify potentially contributing to this exposure by publishing a book? After spending several months considering whether I should scrap my project entirely, wondering all the while if the underlying motives for my research were pure, I eventually came to the conclusion that telling Terlingua's story was important for several reasons.

In the previous chapter, I described how most Terlingua residents have accepted that change is inevitable and that the best way to deal with it is to direct the process of change in a way that preserves what is special about Terlingua. With this in mind, I believe *On the Porch* can play a role in helping to articulate the elements of Terlingua life that residents most cherish, which in turn might help locals as they attempt to promote those characteristics in the future. In the unlikely event that anyone reads this book and decides to move to Terlingua, perhaps a better understanding of their new home will encourage them to approach their move more mindfully, armed with newfound awareness of Terlingua's long-standing values and the discussions that are already taking place concerning the town's growth.

I also believe it is imperative in our current social and political moment to share real stories about life along the US-Mexico border. American citizens, particularly those without personal experience of the borderlands, deserve to understand that the border region is not a lawless war zone and that its residents do not live under constant threat of violence as the news often depicts. They should appreciate that the two thousand-mile-long border is not a single place but many places and that a policy that works for one area does not necessarily fit another. Blanket proposals to build walls or limit border crossings have very real and often devastating consequences for residents on *both* sides of the US-Mexico border. We owe it to these people to be more mindful of the diversity of their experiences and to craft more locally oriented policies that recognize the inherent variety of borderlands culture. Of course, my account also reveals that social and cultural divisions between Anglo and Hispanic residents do exist, even in places like Terlingua where the border has historically been extremely fluid. By acknowledging these divisions in a way that does not point fingers or cast blame, I hope that this book might provide a starting point for conversations about how we all can work to make our communities more inclusive, wherever in the country or the world they happen to exist.

Finally, I believe that we as a nation can learn something valuable from Terlingua when it comes to music. As I have discussed at length, mainstream American society does not have a successful track record when it comes to supporting amateur music making, especially among people who have never been singled out as musically "talented." However, a lifetime of experience has convinced me that there are a great many people in this country who would cherish the opportunity to participate in music, if only someone would provide them the space and encouragement to learn. Unfortunately, even those who have had the benefit of formal music schooling often do not receive the kind of training that would allow them to become musicians for life. I recall my own experience in public school music programs, where music was almost entirely competition-driven and where most students were taught to do one thing and one thing only: read music on the page. Most of my peers in school band and orchestra never again made music after graduating, not because they lost interest, but because they were never taught how to be musicians outside the context of a formal school ensemble.

Terlingua's success at promoting musical participation across a wide range of ability levels clearly demonstrates that an alternative model is possible. With this in mind, I offer some suggestions for music educators and facilitators to consider. First, rather than always segregating musicians based on ability level, consider setting aside time at regular intervals for students of all ability levels to play together. Teachers should also be expected to play alongside their students, rather than simply looking over their shoulders and telling them what they're doing right or wrong. These opportunities would be tremendously beneficial for less experienced students while also encouraging an important mental shift regarding how we think about music as a society. Second, teach improvisation and playing by ear from the very beginning of a young musician's journey. While learning to read musical notation is certainly an important skill, unless you make a career as a classical musician, the vast majority of performance opportunities in the "real world" are not based on reading notation. Learning by ear and improvising without reference to sheet music are far more important abilities for most lifelong musicians. Finally, teach music as a journey, not as a product. Sounding good has its value, but not all music has to be intended for an outside listening audience. The pleasure of creating music for yourselves is enough.

In making these suggestions, I am not arguing for a wholesale paradigm shift in how we as a society teach and think about music. However, if we believe, as I do, that encouraging greater participation in music is a goal worthy of pursuing, we can stand to learn a lot from what Terlingua is doing right. One of my greatest hopes in writing this book is that someone reading these words might see what is happening in the Big Bend and feel empowered to embark on their own musical journey, with no apologies for how they might sound and free of the culturally inscribed notion that only certain "talented" people are worthy of experiencing the absolute joy that is making music.

AS THIS BOOK draws to a close, I recall the words of Terlingua musician Pat O'Bryan as he reflected on the growth of Terlingua's music scene: *What, exactly, is Terlingua music?* It is a fair question given the volume of musical expression in the town. Terlingua music is performed in a wide range of contexts, from non-commercial settings like porches and campfires to commercial venues like the Starlight. From closed-door sessions in the recording studio to open-air concerts on the banks of the Rio Grande. It is characterized by a plethora of genre influences as diverse as the people who perform them, while an ever-rotating cast of characters ensures that the scene never gets too stale. It is impossible, in other words, to encapsulate Terlingua music within one particular setting, person, group, or style.

If all Terlingua music can be united under a single banner, it is the banner of community. Community provides subject matter for local songwriters like Carol and Trevor as they strive to depict their town in verse. It informs opinions about the Porch, the Starlight, and the music that is performed in both. The spirit of community is the guiding principle that allows beginners to jam with pros. It even shapes how residents respond to the growing influx of Austin musicians, forcing them to ask difficult questions about whom their music scene should serve. Each May on the Rio Grande, Terlingua musicians make music with their neighbors across the river, reclaiming a sense of binational community while dancing in a narrow strip of muddy brown water. Even when unthinkable tragedy strikes, local musicians are there, coming together and offering their songs to show what the community spirit is all about.

Of course, none of this is to say that the ideal of community that is espoused by Terlingua residents is always perfectly achieved. This too is sometimes evident in local music. Close examination reveals that, despite assertions to the contrary, hierarchies do exist between Terlingua musicians, even in ostensibly egalitarian settings such as the Porch. Terlingua women still have to fight for opportunities to perform in ways that their male counterparts do not. Finally, the fractured nature of Terlinguan social life—including the noticeable lack of Mexican residents participating in the Ghost Town social scene—raises questions about how comprehensive Terlingua's shared community sentiment truly is.

In the end, this tension between the actual and the ideal serves to reveal Terlingua's truest essence: in a tiny remote border town, a menagerie of desert dwellers from a variety of backgrounds struggle daily to find community in the midst of a changing world. Terlingua music, in all its beauty and imperfection, is a manifestation of this struggle. It is the quest for community expressed in sound.

AS MY RESEARCH drew to a close, I was left wondering what the future holds for the Terlingua community and their music. What will their musical landscape look like five years from now or ten years from now? Terlingua is rapidly becoming recognized as a destination for music. As the number and the skill level of local performers continue to rise, I expect that Terlingua will eventually become a destination for audiences as well. The local population continues to grow, and it is only a matter of time before additional venues open. Certainly, the number of musicians going into the recording studio is only going to increase. When I arrived in Terlingua, the town only had one studio. In the years since, two more local musicians have set up their own spaces for recording, and another two are building studios on "Terlingua time."

As Terlingua's musical population grows, I am curious to see whether the variety of music will grow as well. The impressive but limited pool of musicians who were present during my time in Terlingua meant that dance bands were difficult to form, but it also led to instrumental and stylistic combinations that might not have otherwise occurred. With more musicians in town, dance music might again become a regular part of Terlingua life; however, this might also lead to more conventional instrumentation and fewer opportunities for musicians like me to perform in previously inaccessible styles.

Many other unanswered questions remain concerning Terlingua's future. The town's population is certain to continue growing, but how big can it truly get in such a remote location? How high can the cost of living realistically be expected to increase, and what will be the financial tipping point for Terlingua's creative class? What role will music play in Terlinguan social life as the town's population and infrastructure continue to grow, and how might the local approach to music making change? Will a new generation of resident musicians take up the mantle of those who came before? If so, will they value the same kinds of musical experiences that their forebears did? Finally, and perhaps most importantly, what will happen to Terlingua's cherished community spirit moving forward?

These were the questions on my mind as I drove out to Mark Lewis's house a few weeks before I was to leave Terlingua. Mark was renting a house on the edge of an arroyo, a little ways out on the vast fissured plain north of the Ghost Town. Getting there required a high-clearance vehicle and a drive down a roller coaster of a dirt road that was occasionally impassable during the flash floods that carve through the desert each summer. His house was the only building at the end of a long two-track called Dung Beetle Lane. Naturally, there was no sign at the intersection; according to Mark, the owner of the property only named the road because the state required her to have an official address. From the front porch of the house, Mark could see the entire stretch of Dung Beetle. He was waiting on his porch to greet me when I arrived.

We shook hands and I followed him inside to the kitchen of the small two-room house, lugging along my guitar and a handheld recorder. I had come to conduct one final interview, but we usually ended up playing some music whenever we were together. I set my gear on the floor and took a seat at the kitchen table while Mark walked to the stove at the other end of the room.

"You eaten yet?" he asked me. "How 'bout a bowl of stew?" One of Mark's staple meals involves cooking up a big pot of green chile stew. It's something he picked up from fellow river guides who spent their summers running rivers in New Mexico where green chilies are a staple of regional cuisine. Mark struck a match and lit the burner under a large pot that had already been sitting on the stove when I arrived. "Lately, it's been cool enough that I can just leave it out on the stove. You just gotta make sure you boil it good once a day, as long as it doesn't get too hot outside."

Sharing food is a big thing for Mark. Whenever he talks about good people and good places, he is always referencing "people getting fed." "Delia's is starting to become a thing," he once remarked in reference to a burgeoning local hangout. "She's got showers there, and people are getting fed." As long as I've known Mark, he has always offered to feed me. It quickly became clear that the symbolic act of sharing food is an important part of what community means to him.

Mark left the stove and walked over to the corner where he kept his fiddle. "Why don't we go outside?" he asked. "That stew'll take a while to heat up, and it's a *beautiful* morning today." We grabbed our instruments and headed out to the porch where there was a gorgeous view of the Chisos and Christmas Mountains to the east. It was late morning and still cool, and there was a slight breeze, with just enough humidity in the air to give the creosote bushes their familiar smell of rain. Just beyond his porch to our right, a covey of scaled quail chirped as they darted back and forth over the edge of the arroyo. I turned on my recorder and we began.

Our interview that day was sprawling, as were many of my interviews in Terlingua. We jumped back and forth from one topic to another, allowing the conversation to drift where it would, taking a break every now and then to play a few tunes. Mark told me about running rivers and about what the Ghost Town was like back when Far Flung Adventures was still running raft trips from the Porch. He told me about having campfire jams under the stars among the still-abandoned ruins and about a trip down the river when the scream of a mountain lion echoed through the canyon and sent shivers down his spine. We talked about a friend in town who loved to sing but who had never made music with other people. Mark had recently been singing duets with him out of an old gospel hymnbook.

"Catfish told me that guy *loves* to sing," Mark said. "So you know, I got him over here one day, and we sat around, drank some beer, and he looked through that book and said, 'I can sing that one.' And he started singin' 'Down to the River to Pray.' And I knew the words and he knew all the words, and I said, 'Well, there's our first song.' And I taught him, you know, 'We're gonna sing the melody in unison until we both know exactly what the melody is, and then I can harmonize with you.' And he went home and he *nailed* it, locked it down so he could sing the melody and stay on it, and let people sing harmony around it. We did that for the first time in public yesterday. And I know that man's life was changed. I tell you what, you should get *his* interview."

After a while, the conversation drifted to how the musical climate in Terlingua had changed during Mark's years in town. "The style hasn't changed that much 'cause all you gotta do is hear Collie to hear that style, all you gotta do is hear Chris Baker and you hear that style. All you gotta do

. . ." As Mark was speaking, a low audible rumble began to emerge out of nowhere, faint at first but growing steadily in volume. I looked out at the sky to see a small passenger jet flying low over the Ghost Town, heading southwest toward the Lajitas Golf Resort. It was one of the first flights in a new wave of commercial air traffic into the Lajitas resort from Austin, Houston, and Dallas—the first commercial flights ever to be offered into the Big Bend. The low rumble of the jet grew into a roar, and within seconds it had become so loud that it began to drown out Mark's voice on my recorder.

"Look," Mark yelled over the din, as he stood up from his seat and leaned out over the edge of the Porch. "It's the commercial air traffic, it's just begun. This is the biggest change in Terlingua in a long time, and it's comin' right by for you to take a picture. That just started a week ago, week and a half ago. That's the biggest change ever." I commented that the plane seemed to be flying surprisingly low to the ground, even given its approach into nearby Lajitas. "That was very intentional," Mark replied. "We're now on a scenic tour from Dallas. And they're all sittin' there at the windows, lookin' down at Terlingua for the very first time, pickin' out the Porch and finding out that you and I are there playing music on a regular basis. *If you wanna see somethin' good, go watch the musicians on the Porch on Sunday afternoon.* That's what we are now, we're another roadside attraction. That's what Terlingua is today. It's no longer a river town, it's another roadside attraction. I don't like what's going on, but there's nothing I can *do* about it, so I just have to try to keep my mouth shut, but . . ."

Mark paused and asked me to turn off the recorder for a while, saying he needed to take a break. The flyover had obviously been a powerful symbol of change, just one more in a seemingly endless string of such moments that punctuate life in Terlingua. I had heard many residents express frustration about the flyovers in recent months. After witnessing one for myself, I could see why people were upset.

Mark sat back down and picked up my guitar while the roar of the jet engines continued overhead. But as the plane passed over the Ghost Town and disappeared into the distance toward Lajitas, its rumbling grew steadily fainter until it was eventually overtaken by the silence of the desert it left behind. The only sounds that remained were the wind whistling softly through the arroyo, and a covey of chirping quail, and a guitar being tuned, and the soft whine of a propane stove with a pot of stew just beginning to come to a boil.

ACKNOWLEDGMENTS

NO PROJECT OF THIS SIZE could be completed without the assistance of a large supporting cast, and this book is no exception. *On the Porch* began as a PhD dissertation, and I received a tremendous amount of feedback in the early stages of the project from my dissertation committee members, Jay Keister, Carlo Caballero, Carla Jones, Austin Okigbo, and Brenda Romero. Mary Diesel, Emjay Holmes, and Thomas Turino also provided invaluable input at different stages of the writing process. I am especially grateful to Carlo Caballero and Elissa Guralnick, whose unflagging encouragement continued to propel me forward even when I did not believe myself capable of writing a book. I thank the Graduate School and the College of Music at the University of Colorado Boulder for their financial assistance during my early periods of fieldwork and writing. Finally, I thank my editor at the University of Texas Press, Casey Kittrell, for the vision he brought to bear on this project and for his tireless efforts in seeing it through to the finish line.

I am indebted to many teachers and mentors who have guided me during my lifelong journey as a musician, among them Bert Bostic, Vivian Moss, Debbie O'Brien, Michael Jacobson, and Alex Parker. I am grateful to Mark Parker for introducing me to campfire music at a young age and for instilling in me a passion for Texas singer-songwriters that ultimately inspired me to pursue research in Texas. I would also like to thank Alfredo Colman and the late Richard "Doc" Evans for their formative guidance and friendship during my undergraduate years.

A long list of friends have provided me with advice, fellowship, and good humor along the journey; among them are Michael Harris, Jenna Palensky, Teresita Lozano, Kevin and Heather Muirhead, Shannon O'Connell, and Estella

Cumberford. Jamie Aponte provided good company and much appreciated translation assistance. I also thank Bruno Petersons and the late Larry Fisher for being unfailingly flexible as I attempted to fit my work schedule around my research and writing schedule.

For their unwavering love and support, I thank my parents, Bruce and Alison Peeler, my siblings, Madison and Zane Peeler, and my grandparents, Ken and LaVoe Peeler and Bill and Alice Wright. I owe an additional debt of gratitude to my grandparents, Bill and Alice Wright, for instilling a lifelong love of the Big Bend region in their children and grandchildren.

Finally, and above all, I would like to thank the people of Terlingua, Texas. Some of their names grace these pages but many more do not. They are far too numerous to mention here individually, but without their support, cooperation, and friendship, this story would have been impossible to tell. From my first days in Terlingua, they welcomed me into their lives and into their music. I am eternally grateful.

NOTES

PROLOGUE: ON THE PORCH

1. This observation was previously made by Blair Pittman, a longtime Porch-sitter and chronicler of Terlingua, in his book *Tales From the Terlingua Porch* (Wimberley, TX: Sun Country Publications, 2005), iii.

INTRODUCTION: HUNDRED MILES FROM NOWHERE

1. Locals use the terms "Terlingua," "South Brewster County," and "South County" more or less interchangeably, a practice I adhere to throughout the course of this book.
2. "The Yippee-I-Ay Song" by Jim Keaveny. All rights reserved by the songwriter.
3. "Terlingua Blues" by Randy Moore. All rights reserved by the songwriter.
4. "West Texas Night" by Greg Grymes. All rights reserved by the songwriter.
5. I was also curious if there were any connections between Terlingua and other notable music towns in Texas. Places like Austin, Luckenbach, Gruene, and Kerrville had all developed well-documented music scenes in the 1970s, but nothing had ever been written about Terlingua music as best I could tell.
6. John Blacking, *How Musical Is Man?* (Seattle: University of Washington Press, 1973), 104.

CHAPTER 1: STARLIGHT AND STAGE LIGHTS

1. This original mural was created by Frank X. Tolbert Jr., and it predates the arrival of the first river guides by several years.
2. For a complete account of Terlingua's mining period, see Kenneth Baxter Ragsdale, *Quicksilver: Terlingua and the Chisos Mining Company* (College Station: Texas A&M University Press, 1976).

3. Although the chili cook-offs are an important part of Terlingua history, they do not feature significantly in this book because they are largely imported festivals. The cook-offs are almost exclusively organized, run, and attended by visitors to Terlingua, and most local residents have nothing to do with them.

4. Arthur R. Gómez, *A Most Singular Country: A History of Occupation in the Big Bend* (Provo, UT: Charles Redd Center for Western Studies, Brigham Young University, 1990), 1; John Jameson, *The Story of Big Bend National Park* (Austin: University of Texas Press, 1996), 12; United States National Park Service Division of Publications, *Big Bend: Official National Park Handbook* (Washington, DC: US Department of the Interior, 1983), 7.

5. Polly W. Wiessner, "Embers of Society: Firelight Talk Among the Ju'hoansi Bushmen," *Proceedings of the National Academy of Sciences* 111, no. 39 (September 2014): 14027. Wiessner is rightfully careful to remind readers that "data from modern foragers cannot be projected back to interpret the distant past. These data can, however, give us a realistic sense of . . . what could be accomplished in a firelit niche, and grounds to formulate questions and hypotheses regarding the impact of firelight on social and cultural evolution."

6. In distinguishing between different varieties of musical performance in Terlingua, I was heavily influenced by the work of Thomas Turino, particularly his book *Music as Social Life: The Politics of Participation* (Chicago: University of Chicago Press, 2008). What I refer to loosely in this book as "gigs" and "jams," Turino refers to as "presentational music" and "participatory music," respectively.

7. Not all forms of jamming are created equal, and Terlingua jams are often looser than their counterparts in other locales. For example, in places where jazz jams and traditional Irish sessions occur, they frequently have their own specific codes of etiquette and expectations for proficiency.

8. I believe that events like the Texas River Music Series are a big part of what has allowed Terlingua to become a popular destination for A-list performers, despite the obvious logistical challenges in performing there. The progressive country music that put Austin on the map (and by which Terlingua music has been significantly

influenced) relies heavily for its success on being perceived as more "authentic" than the Nashville-based pop country out of which it grew. Performances in small towns like Terlingua, Gruene, and Luckenbach thus provide progressive country artists with an important form of cultural capital, a means of demonstrating their authenticity via a tangible connection to rural Texas. Besides, playing music on the river is fun.

9. John Blacking, "Identifying Processes of Musical Change," *The World of Music* 28, no. 1 (1986): 12.

CHAPTER 2: IN THE INCUBATOR

1. Henry Kingsbury, *Music, Talent, and Performance: A Conservatory Cultural System* (Philadelphia: Temple University Press, 1988), 60.

2. John Messenger, "Esthetic Talent," *Basic College Quarterly* 4 (1958): 20–22.

3. Steven Feld, "Sound Structure as Social Structure," *Ethnomusicology* 28, no. 3 (September 1984): 390.

4. Blacking, *How Musical Is Man?*, 34.

5. Ibid., 7.

6. John A. Sloboda, "The Acquisition of Musical Performance Expertise: Deconstructing the 'Talent' Account of Individual Differences in Musical Expressivity," in *The Road to Excellence: The Acquisition of Expert Performance in the Arts and Sciences, Sports and Games*, ed. K. Anders Ericsson (Mahwah, NJ: Lawrence Erlbaum Associates, 1996), 108.

7. Earl Hunt, "Expertise, Talent, and Social Encouragement," in *The Cambridge Handbook of Expertise and Expert Performance*, ed. K. Anders Ericsson, et al. (Cambridge, UK: Cambridge University Press, 2006), 34–35.

8. Christopher Small, *Musicking: The Meanings of Performance and Listening* (Middletown, CT: Wesleyan University Press, 1998), 71–72.

9. For more on the role of technology in the commercial music industry, see David Suisman, *Selling Sounds: The Commercial Revolution in American Music* (Cambridge: Harvard University Press, 2009).

10. Mark Katz, *Capturing Sound: How Technology Has Changed Music*, rev. ed. (Berkeley: University of California Press, 2010), 56–57.

11. Suisman, *Selling Sounds*, 5–11.

12. Richard Crawford and Larry Hamberlin, *An Introduction to America's Music*, 2nd ed. (New York: W. W. Norton, 2013), 171.

13. Suisman, *Selling Sounds*, 91.

14. Ibid., 254; Katz, *Capturing Sound*, 76.

15. Suisman, *Selling Sounds*, 16–17.

16. Small, *Musicking*, 73.

17. Eventually, a few enterprising Terlingua residents began broadcasting their own pirate radio station, called KYOTE Radio, from their headquarters in the Ghost Town, but the Federal Communications Commission eventually caught on and shut them down.

18. An implicit but powerful assumption underlies Collie's quote: that there are certain gendered ways of performing music. Several other female musicians I interviewed also hinted at a belief that masculine and feminine performance styles are fundamentally different, using terms like "loud," "powerful," and "energetic" to describe masculine playing and "soft," "gentle," and "intimate" to describe feminine playing. While it is clear that such culturally imbedded assumptions about gender are powerful factors that shape how people interpret the social act of music making, it must also be acknowledged that no biological basis exists for ascribing such traits by gender. Indeed, there are many musicians, even within the relatively small Terlingua scene, who defy such reductionist categorizations (women who perform music loud and fast and men who perform softly). Esther Terpenning has identified similar ideas about gender-coded performance styles within Irish traditional music in "Gendering the Irish Traditional Flute" (master's thesis, University of Limerick, 2011). For a more detailed examination of gendered musical performance, refer also to Jane C. Sugarman, *Engendering Song: Singing and Subjectivity at Prespa Albanian Weddings* (Chicago: University of Chicago Press, 1997).

CHAPTER 3: THE AUSTIN EFFECT

1. "Dirt and Stone" by Trevor Reichman. All rights reserved by the songwriter.

2. Christopher Gray, "The 2000s: An Introduction," in *The Austin Chronicle Music Anthology*, ed. Austin Powell and Doug Freeman (Austin: University of Texas Press, 2011), 181.

3. Jan Reid, *The Improbable Rise of Redneck Rock* (Austin: University of Texas Press, 2004), 4. For more on Austin's growth as a music destination, see also Joe Nick Patoski, *Austin to ATX: The Hippies, Pickers, Slackers & Geeks Who Transformed the Capital of Texas* (College Station: Texas A&M University Press, 2019); Jason Mellard, *Progressive Country: How the 1970s Transformed the Texan in Popular Culture* (Austin: University of Texas Press, 2014); and Travis Stimeling, *Cosmic Cowboys and New Hicks: The Countercultural Sounds of Austin's Progressive Country Music Scene* (Oxford, UK: Oxford University Press, 2011).

4. Bill Bentley, "At the Starting Gates of the Seventies," *Austin Chronicle*, September 3, 1993, in *The Austin Chronicle Music Anthology*, ed. Austin Powell and Doug Freeman (Austin: University of Texas Press, 2011), 126.

5. Chet Flippo, "Remembering the Cosmic Cowboy Years," *Austin Chronicle*, January 14, 1994, in *The Austin Chronicle Music Anthology*, ed. Austin Powell and Doug Freeman (Austin: University of Texas Press, 2011), 133.

6. Chet Flippo, "Hill Country Sound," *Texas Parade*, April 1974, 16.

7. Ibid., 20.

8. Flippo, "Remembering the Cosmic Cowboy Years," 132.

9. Jan Reid and Don Roth, "The Coming of Redneck Hip," *Texas Monthly*, November 1973, texasmonthly.com/the-culture/the-coming-of-redneck-hip.

10. David Sackllah, "The Crisis of Gentrification Hits the Austin Music Scene," *Pitchfork.com*, July 9, 2015, pitchfork.com/thepitch/836-the-crisis-of-gentrification-hits-the-austin-music-scene. For a local response to the *Pitchfork* article, see *American-Statesman* Staff, "Pitchfork: Austin Music Scene Dealing with 'Crisis of Gentrification'," *Austin360.com*, July 9, 2015, music.blog.austin360.com/2015/07/09/pitch/fork-austin-music-scene-dealing-with-crisis-of-gentrification.

11. ACL began as a weekly PBS show in 1976 and became a festival in 2002, while SXSW was founded in 1987.

12. City of Austin, Economic Development Department, Music and Entertainment Division, *The Austin Music Census:*

A Data-Driven Assessment of Austin's Commercial Music Economy, commissioned by the City of Austin from Titan Music Group, 2015, austintexas.gov/sites/default/files/files/Austin_Music _Census_Interactive_PDF_53115.pdf.

13. It is important to note that Austin has been successful in supporting its resident musicians in ways that many other cities have not. For example, the Health Alliance for Austin Musicians, which was founded in 2005, provides affordable healthcare for area musicians. In addition, the fact that the City of Austin commissioned the Austin Music Census—the first of its kind in any major US city—demonstrates a commitment to addressing the aforementioned issues that has not been matched elsewhere.

14. "Mañanaland" by Alice Knight. All rights reserved by the songwriter.

15. "Traffic" by Trevor Reichman. All rights reserved by the songwriter.

16. Texas Water Development Board, *Frequently Asked Questions*, twdb.texas.gov/innovativewater/rainwater/faq.asp#title-08.

17. US Department of Energy, *Solar Energy Potential*, energy.gov /maps/solar-energy-potential.

18. There is a law in Texas that requires people living off the grid to have functional septic systems. Many Terlingua residents have taken advantage of a state grant for rural residents that covers the cost of installing these systems. For environmental reasons, some people prefer to use composting toilets even after having their septic systems installed.

19. Jeffrey Ellrick Farley, "Culture Industry as Cottage Industry: The Production of Musical Meaning in Austin, Texas" (PhD diss., University of Texas at Austin, 1996), 117.

20. Brian Eckhouse, Ari Natter, and Christopher Martin, "President Trump Slaps Tariffs on Solar Panels in Major Blow to Renewable Energy," *Time*, January 22, 2018, time.com/5113472/donald -trump-solar-panel-tariff.

21. SolarReviews, "How much do solar panels cost in Texas in 2020?" solar-estimate.org/solar-panel-cost/texas.

CHAPTER 4: VOICES FROM BOTH SIDES

1. San Carlos was officially renamed "Manuel Benavides" in 1928, in honor of a former mayor killed during the Mexican

Revolution, but most residents still refer to the town by its earlier name.

2. Dane Keane, "21 Arrested in Border Patrol Roundup at Lajitas Crossing," *International*, May 16, 2002.

3. "Getting Fatter" by Laird Considine. All rights reserved by the songwriter.

4. "Little Green Men" by Bryn Moore. All rights reserved by the songwriter.

5. "Guadalupe" by Alex Whitmore. All rights reserved by the songwriter.

6. "Olé Song" by Trevor Reichman. All rights reserved by the songwriter. Note that the word "mire" here holds double meaning. In a figurative sense, it refers to the stressful and complicated situation that has arisen due to the border closure, while in a literal sense, it refers to meeting in the middle of the Rio Grande during the Voices festival that inspired the song.

7. "Fiesta Protesta" by Jeff Haislip. All rights reserved by the songwriter.

8. US Border Patrol, "Sector Profile—Fiscal Year 2019," cbp.gov /document/stats/us-border-patrol-fiscal-year-2019-sector-profile. For fifty-eight years of statistics on undocumented border crossings by sector, see US Border Patrol, "Southwest Border Sectors," cbp .gov/sites/default/files/assets/documents/2019-Mar/bp-southwest -border-sector-apps-fy1960-fy2018.pdf.

9. "Walls Divide" by Trevor Reichman. All rights reserved by the songwriter.

10. "Chinga Tu Muro" by Tony Drewry. All rights reserved by the songwriter.

11. While I use the terms "Anglo" and "Hispanic" here for the sake of clarity, it is important to recognize that many people of Mexican descent living in the United States prefer the identifier "Mexican," rather than more generic terms such as "Hispanic" and "Latinx," as the latter terms have a tendency to conflate groups of people with sometimes vastly different ethnic or national origins.

CHAPTER 5: GETTING FATTER

1. Life in Terlingua is full of these symbolic celebrations of differentness. One of my favorites is the local tradition of "inverted fireworks." Terlingua residents periodically gather at night

to light fireworks, but they don't shoot them into the air as most people do. Instead, they go to one of the abandoned mine shafts scattered around the Ghost Town and lie facedown on top of the large metal grate that covers the hole. Then, while suspended above eight hundred feet of empty air, they shoot the fireworks straight down into the earth, each one briefly illuminating the mine shaft walls section by section as it rockets down into the blackness. Inverted fireworks are a rite of passage in Terlingua, one of the rare activities in a tourist town in which only local residents participate, and the symbolism is not arbitrary. By intentionally subverting the normal use of fireworks—like the normal direction for watching a sunset—in such a deliberate and celebratory way, Terlinguans are articulating their collective identity as distinct, and even opposite, from mainstream American society.

2. "Getting Fatter" by Laird Considine. All rights reserved by the songwriter.

3. Rachel Monroe, "A Murder in Terlingua, Texas," *Outside*, May 6, 2014, outsideonline.com/adventure-travel/north-america/united-states/texas/Murder-in-Texas-Hardest-Partying-Ghost-Town.html.

4. Christopher Hooks, "¿Viva Terlingua?" *Texas Monthly*, April 2014, texasmonthly.com/travel/viva-terlingua.

5. For more on Marfa's transformation, see Kathleen Shafer, *Marfa: The Transformation of a West Texas Town* (Austin: University of Texas Press, 2017).

6. In this respect, the political relationship between the Ghost Town and the outlying areas of South Brewster County parallels that between urban and suburban America or between urban and rural America more broadly—more liberal at the center, more conservative at the margins.

7. Sam Howe Verhovek, "Another Day, Another 89 Miles to School," *New York Times*, December 9, 1994, nytimes.com/1994/12/09/us/another-day-another-89-miles-to-school.html.

8. Hooks, "¿Viva Terlingua?"

9. Monroe, "A Murder in Terlingua, Texas."

INDEX